T0328526

Cambridge Elements ≡

Elements in Beckett Studies
edited by
Dirk Van Hulle
University of Oxford
Mark Nixon
University of Reading

BECKETT AND SADE

Jean-Michel Rabaté
University of Pennsylvania

CAMBRIDGE
UNIVERSITY PRESS

CAMBRIDGE
UNIVERSITY PRESS

University Printing House, Cambridge CB2 8BS, United Kingdom

One Liberty Plaza, 20th Floor, New York, NY 10006, USA

477 Williamstown Road, Port Melbourne, VIC 3207, Australia

314–321, 3rd Floor, Plot 3, Splendor Forum, Jasola District Centre, New Delhi – 110025, India

79 Anson Road, #06–04/06, Singapore 079906

Cambridge University Press is part of the University of Cambridge.

It furthers the University's mission by disseminating knowledge in the pursuit of education, learning, and research at the highest international levels of excellence.

www.cambridge.org
Information on this title: www.cambridge.org/9781108726832
DOI: 10.1017/9781108771085

© Jean-Michel Rabaté 2020

First published 2020

A catalogue record for this publication is available from the British Library.

ISBN 978-1-108-72683-2 Paperback
ISSN 2632–0746 (online)
ISSN 2632–0738 (print)

Beckett and Sade

Elements in Beckett Studies

DOI: 10.1017/9781108771085
First published online: October 2020

Jean-Michel Rabaté
University of Pennsylvania

Author for correspondence: Jean-Michel Rabaté, jmrabate@english.upenn.edu

Abstract: Much has been written on Beckett and Sade, yet nothing systematic has been produced. This Element is systematic by adopting a chronological order, which is necessary given the complexity of Beckett's varying assessments of Sade. Beckett mentioned Sade early in his career, with Proust as a first guide. His other sources were Guillaume Apollinaire, and Mario Praz's book, *La carne, la morte e il diavolo nella letteratura romantica* (1930), from which he took notes about sadism for his *Dream Notebook*. Dante's meditation on the absurdity of justice provides closure, facing Beckett's wonder at the pervasive presence of sadism in humans.

Keywords: sadism, torture, the Revolution, ethics, politics

ISBNs: 9781108726832 (PB), 9781108771085 (OC)
ISSNs: 2632-0746 (online), 2632-0738 (print)

Contents

Introduction: The Sade Boom

Beckett kept a keen interest in the works and person of the Marquis de Sade all his life. Quite late, he became conscious that he had participated in a 'Sade boom', dating from the inception of French Surrealism, from Guillaume Apollinaire, André Breton and Georges Bataille to the explosion of Sadean scholarship in the 1950s. Even if Beckett realized that he had been caught up in a Sade cult, he never abjured his faith in the importance of the outcast and scandalous writer, and kept rereading Sade (as he did Dante) across the years.[1] I will begin by surveying Beckett's letters to find the traces of his readings and point out how a number of hypotheses concerning the 'divine Marquis' evolved over time. Beckett revisited Sade several times, and he progressively reshaped and refined his interpretation of what Sade meant for him across five decades. Following the evolution of these epistolary markers that culminated in a more political reading, I will distinguish four moments in Beckett's approach.

Beckett knew the details of Sade's exceptional life, a life that was not a happy one but was certainly a long one, for his career spanned the Old Regime, the French Revolution and almost all of the First Empire. Sade was jailed for debauchery from 1777 to 1790, then imprisoned for a short time at the height of the Terror in 1793–4, which allowed him to witness the mass slaughter; he was freed just before the date set for his execution, thanks to Robespierre's downfall; he was jailed again for his pornographic writings under the Consulate and the Empire under direct orders from a puritanical Napoleon, between 1801 and 1814. He died in the Charenton asylum, where he was kept under the pretence that he was insane. The authorities knew very well that he was a subversive writer but considered him a pornographer even though his writings were more emetic than titillating or erotic. Altogether Sade spent twenty-seven years in prison, quite a record for a nobleman from an ancient and distinguished family who had never killed anyone. Sade was aware that the imposition of force on his passions had not restrained them but on the contrary exacerbated their violence. Indeed, Sade's scandalous reiterations of perverse fantasies go beyond the limits of what is considered as sayable. Feeling sympathy for this accused martyr who had produced a radical form of literature, Beckett recognized the importance of the dire lessons on love, sexuality and power contained in Sade's sulphurous works.

The first mention of Sade comes from a 1934 letter revealing Beckett's sense that the Marquis de Sade's influence had permeated the cultural world of the Dublin intelligentsia, a world in which eccentrics and perverts were hard to

---

[1] See Eric Marty's critical and perceptive book, *Pourquoi le XXe siècle a-t-il pris Sade au sérieux?* (2011). For a comprehensive assessment of Beckett's interest in Sade's works, see Pilling (2014).

distinguish. This satirical moment corresponds to the unpublished novel *Dream of Fair to Middling Women*, Beckett's farewell to his student years in Dublin and Paris. It brings us to the moment of intense rumination preceding the writing of *Murphy*, when he was elaborating an aesthetic of non-anthropomorphic values. This comes to the fore in a letter to MacGreevy from September 1934; Beckett praises Cézanne for his paintings of Montagne Sainte Victoire, a landscape rendered 'incommensurable with all human expressions whatsoever' (2009, 222), adding:

> Could there be any more ludicrous rationalisation of the itch to animise than the état d'âme balls, banquets & parties. Or – after Xerxes beating the sea, the Lexicographer kicking the stone & the Penman under the bed during the thunder – any irritation more mièvre than that of Sade at the impossibilité d'outrager la nature. A.E.'s Gully would have thrilled him. (Beckett, 2009, 223)

Here, Sade's 'irritation' is presented as *mièvre*, which suggests something soft and effeminate, hardly what one would expect from the Marquis! In 1934, Sade can be compared with those Irish artists who still appeal to an anthropomorphized nature, whereas Cézanne's strength was that he presented it as inhuman. This allusion to Sade follows an ironical evocation of James Joyce, whose terror of thunderstorms was legendary. Beckett had found in Mario Praz Sade's statement that 'L'impossibilité d'outrager la nature est, selon moi, le plus grand supplice de l'homme [The impossibility of outraging Nature is, according to me, man's greatest torment]' (Sade, 1967b, 281; Praz, 1948, 109).[2] This quote is taken out of its context; we find it in *La Nouvelle Justine*, spoken by Jérome, one of the Libertines, the oldest of a group of ferocious monks. Jérome likes being whipped or sodomized when engaging in his main activity, which is torturing to death little girls and boys. Jérome is one among many Sadean antiheroes who all express a demiurgic urge to commit crimes so extravagant that they will have no equivalent in the annals of human debauchery; they are ready to destroy the whole human race, if not the world. However, here Beckett betrays a second-hand knowledge, for he lifted the sentence from Praz's *The Romantic Agony*.

At the time, Praz was developing a groundbreaking concept of decadence that took Sade as the hidden source both of a darker neo-Gothic Romanticism and of an enervated and affected late Symbolism (Praz, 1948, 107).[3] Praz finished writing his book in 1930, just when Maurice Heine was publishing the first

---

[2] *La Nouvelle Justine* is an expanded version, published in 1797, of *Justine, ou les malheurs de la vertu* from 1791. Unless otherwise noted, all translations are the author's own.

[3] Praz attributes this sentence to Sade and not to the character who uttered it, Jérome.

scholarly edition of one of Sade's works, *Justine*. Beckett read Praz's book in Italian, as his notes in the *Dream Notebook* reveal (Beckett, 1999, 45).[4] He was attracted to its chapter on Sade not only because it quotes Sade in French and quite extensively, but also because Praz establishes a direct link between Sade and Proust, which gave useful tips to Beckett at the time when he was writing his monograph *Proust* (1970; published 1931). Like Praz, Beckett had been impressed by the numerous passages devoted to 'sadism' in Proust's *Recherche*, and his book highlighted the startling absence of moral condemnation of any form of 'perversion'.

In the letter, the tone is mocking, almost sarcastic. Sade's destructive fury is reduced to an insane rage at nature, a frustrated wish to be one with elemental destructivity. This looked immature to Beckett in 1934, precisely when he was taking some distance both from the Dublin aesthetes and from his main artistic mentor, Joyce. The Sadean drive reminds him of the pleasure taken by Leonardo da Vinci in *disfazione*, a term mentioned in his *Proust* (Beckett, 1970, 31). *Disfazione* or 'decreation' implies the artist's enjoyment of destruction, whether it be in Nature or in man-made catastrophes. This tendency appeared, as Beckett found out later, in the works of André Masson and Georges Bataille. Indeed, after World War II, he would mock Bataille's proclivity for 'all-purpose disaster'.[5]

In the 1934 letter, the allusion to Sade segues into an ironical remark on a kitschy painting by George Russell, a.k.a. AE, whose *Seascape: The Gully* was part of the Hugh Lane bequest in the Dublin museum. If the adjective *mièvre* (simpering) hardly qualifies when dealing with Sade's murderous frenzies in *Justine*, it is more fitting facing AE's daub, in which two women seated on a rock enjoy the wild surge of the surf. While the satirical tone reappears in other evocations of Sade in *Dream*, in the passages to which I will return, the remark betrays Beckett's lack of familiarity with Sade's works.

In a second period, Beckett began considering Sade's texts more closely and with the idea of a serious task ahead, which included translation but also scholarly glosses. The task was forced on him when he was given the offer by Jack Kahane to translate Sade's most shocking book, *The 120 Days of Sodom*. Beckett was tempted for many reasons, and in February 1938, he pondered whether to translate it, asking George Reavey for advice:

---

[4] Beckett quotes 'Nastàja Filippovna', a character in Dostoyevsky's *The Idiot*, using Praz's spelling, whereas the English version was 'Nastasia'. This proves that Beckett read Praz in Italian, in the first edition, just published then.

[5] Beckett uses the amusing expression 'désastre à tout faire' in an undated letter of 1950 to Georges Duthuit (2011, 186). I have discussed their growing disagreement in *Think, Pig!* (Rabaté, 2016, 76–91).

I wish very much you were here to advise me about translation (of Sade's 120 Days for Jack Kahane). I should like very much to do it, & the terms are moderately satisfactory, but don't know what effect it wd. have on my lit. situation in England or how it might prejudice future publications of my own there. The surface is of an unheard of obscenity & not 1 in 100 will find literature in the pornography, or beneath the pornography, let alone one of the capital works of the 18th century, which it is for me. (Beckett, 2009, 604)

On 11 February 1938, shortly after a stay in a hospital after he had been stabbed near the heart, he still hesitated, even if the proposition appealed to him. He mentions his long-standing interest in Sade: 'Though I am interested in Sade & have been for a long time, and want the money badly, I would really rather not' (605, n4). He proceeded to formulate his most original statement about Sade in another letter:

[Jack Kahane] agreed to the following conditions: 1. That I shall write the preface. 2. That I should be paid 150 fr per 1000 words irrespective of rate of £. (. . .) I have read 1st & 3rd vols. of French edition. The obscenity of surface is indescribable. Nothing could be less pornographical. It fills me with a kind of metaphysical ecstasy. The composition is extraordinary, as rigorous as Dante's. If the dispassionate statement of 600 'passions' is Puritan and a complete absence of satire juvenalesque, then it is, as you say, puritanical & juvenalesque. You would loathe it whether or no. (21 February 1938; Beckett, 2009, 607)

Beckett alludes to the plan of Sade's darkest and most haunting novel, *The 120 Days of Sodom*, a frenzied book written in thirty-seven days in 1785 while he was imprisoned in the Bastille. Sade wrote it on pages glued together in a huge reel and in a minute script. Despite these precautions, Sade was forced to leave his cell, and lost the manuscript; he lamented its disappearance all his life. The manuscript was to resurface only in 1904, when it was published by a German scholar. After having been the object of ferocious legal battles between French and Swiss institutions, it is now kept in Paris, and has been shown several times.[6] It was called a *bande* by Sade, with a pun on *bander* (to have an erection), which may have suggested the French title of *Krapp's Last Tape*, *La dernière bande*.

In Sade's Gothic dystopia, four rich libertines decide to spend four months in a secluded castle in the Black Forest in order to act out their most violent fantasies. The Castle of Silling resembles Sade's castle of La Coste, to which I will return in the context of Beckett's stay in nearby Roussillon during the war. The Libertines take with them four old bawds who act as narrators for scenes

---

[6] It was one of the attractions on display at the show *L'Enfer de la Bibliothèque: Eros au secret*, Bibliothèque nationale de France, site François-Mitterrand, 4 December 2007 to 31 March 2008.

that are staged and performed with living people; they are helped by a group of strong men who assist them when they subdue, rape, torment and kill thirty-six victims, all young men and women. Four months are spent exploring six hundred passions that are divided into four types: the simple, the complex, the criminal and the murderous passions. At the end, all the remaining victims are dispatched quickly. For a while Sade had believed in numerology. We find complex calculations in his books. This calculating method has its equivalent in many passages of *Watt*. In his assessment, Beckett links Sade's masterpiece with the system of divine punishments in Dante's *Inferno*. He is alluding to the new edition in three volumes, *Les 120 journées de Sodome, ou l'école du libertinage*, that Maurice Heine published from 1931 to 1935.

In a letter of 8 March 1938, Beckett announces that he has accepted the offer to do the translation (2009, 610). His Dublin friend Con Leventhal was visiting Paris and was eager to have Beckett publish an essay on Sade: 'He hopes to place an article by me on the divine marquise [*sic*] in Hermathena of all places, where by the way Miss MacCarthy has suddenly begun to translate from Stefan Georg [*sic*]' (622). By shifting George's final *e* to 'marquis', in what may not have been a double slip of the pen, is Beckett poking fun at the Marquis's bisexual orientation in this feminization of the name, or is he already patroniz-ing the restaurant that would be his regular haunt for decades, the fish place with excellent Beaujolais wine, 'Aux îles Marquises', situated at 15, rue de la Gaîté, near the main theatres of Montparnasse?[7] After all, the Marquis de Sade was born on the spot occupied by another of Beckett's favourite restaurants, Le Cochon de Lait, at 7, rue Corneille, very close to the famous Odéon theatre, as he notes in 1951 (see Beckett, 2011, 224).

Despite these facetious asides, Beckett remained cautious about the transla-tion. His prudence was motivated by the not-unfounded worry that if he associated his name with that of Sade, he would be branded as a pornographer. His unfortunate choice of a title such as *More Pricks Than Kicks* had already produced negative effects during the trial in which he appeared as a witness against Oliver Gogarty in Dublin, even though he and his family won the case (see Knowlson, 1996, 257–9). Had Beckett chosen to associate himself with Jack Kahane and the Obelisk Press then, he would have been lumped with authors like Henry Miller (*Tropic of Cancer*, 1934), Anaïs Nin (*House of Incest*, 1936) and Lawrence Durrell (*The Black Book*, 1938). Ironically, he ended up being associated with similarly censored publishers after the war: Maurice Girodias (Olympia Press), John Calder (Calder Press) and

---

[7] A letter from January 1952, to which I will return, mentions side by side Sade's *120 journées* and the Iles Marquises restaurant (Beckett, 2011, 309–10).

Barney Rosset (Grove Press). When Girodias published *Watt* in Paris, Beckett's book was advertised along with *Plexus* by Henry Miller. Then Girodias published the first English version of Sade's *Philosophy in the Bedroom* (see St. Jorre, 1994, 53–7).[8]

A third period comes immediately after the war, when Beckett translated, for Georges Duthuit's second *Transition* journal, not only Sade but also texts by the main editor of Sade's texts, Maurice Heine. Beckett also appreciated the essays penned by the most intelligent commentator of Sade, Maurice Blanchot. Reading these subtle critical analyses with a view to translating them led to an immersion in books by Sade and on Sade. In December 1950, Beckett wrote to Duthuit about the excellent book by Maurice Blanchot, *Lautréamont et Sade*, published in 1949:

> I have read Blanchot's *Sade*. There are some very good things in it. A few tremendous quotations that I did not know, in the style of the one I knocked up for you from the *120 Days*. Hard to single out one passage to translate, but I managed to and started on it. . . . Maybe we could spice things up by putting in a few extracts from Klossowski [*Sade mon prochain*] and Maurice Heine [foreword to the *Dialogue entre un prêtre et un moribond*]. The passage already translated from *Philosophie dans le Boudoir* is not too bad, but there are better ones to be found. (Beckett, 2011, 211)

In the same letter, Beckett expresses annoyance because he has discovered that Marcel Jouhandeau had published a *Godeau intime* in 1926. For a while, he looked for another name as the title of his major French play (Beckett, 2011, 210–11). Jouhandeau, who had chosen the camp of the collaborators during the war, had published a first essay on 'abjection' in the *Nouvelle Revue Française* in 1938. Jouhandeau was offering an apology of evil that implicitly looked back to Sadean principles; the choice of Godeau for Jouhandeau's anti-hero, as we see in *Monsieur Godeau marié* (1933), almost forced Beckett to reconsider his choice of a French name that barely distorted the idea of an 'abject God'. But Jouhandeau was too much of a perverted Catholic to interest Beckett. What stands out in the conversation with Duthuit is Beckett's predilection for Blanchot's analyses and his respect for the scholarship of Maurice Heine in the latter's groundbreaking introduction, *Le Marquis de Sade*:

> I have finished the Blanchot. It makes 12 pages of text. Some excellent ideas, or rather starting-points for ideas, and a fair bit of verbiage, to be read quickly, not as a translator does. What emerges from it though is a truly gigantic Sade, jealous of Satan and of his eternal torments, and confronting nature more than

---

[8] S. E. Gontarski has insisted on the concept of a 'decadent Beckett' (2018, 1–32).

human-kind. ... We could put in too the end that I read you, about the disappearance of his body. (Beckett, 2011, 219)

The last sentence alludes to Sade's famous testament, in which he indicated his wish to be buried in an unmarked spot in a wood and have acorns planted on it so that his memory would be erased from the earth. Beckett then plunged into Sade's correspondence and the rapidly growing secondary literature on Sade:

> I have translated 4 letters by Sade (one of them extremely beautiful), cutting down as far as possible the rubbish Lely writes as linking material. All the rest of the work he has given you seems pointless and unusable. The so-called notes on the death-penalty make no mention of it. For that you would have to go to Sade himself, probably *Philosophy in the Bedroom*. (Beckett, 2011, 222)

We do not know for sure which letters Beckett is referring to here; it is likely that he is thinking of the famous letters Sade sent to his mother-in-law, the Présidente de Montreuil, who persecuted her son-in-law relentlessly, and those he sent to his wife; in the latter, he pours scorn on the idea that locking him up in a cell can do him any good. In a letter from March 1777, he accuses his enemies of wanting to 'bestialize his soul', fearing as a consequence of imprisonment the 'dreadful disorder' he feels 'brewing in his mind' (Sade, 1965, 128). In a letter from 25 June 1783, he warns that because of his constant incarceration, a 'ferment' has been produced in his brain: 'owing to you phantoms have arisen in me which I shall have to render real' (134). Beckett must have pondered these famous words: 'Vous m'avez fait former des fantômes qu'il faudra que je réalise'. This might serve as a motto for Beckett. Sade had discussed the death penalty in the fifth dialogue of *Philosophy in the Bedroom* and, surprisingly, was opposed to it, a point to which we will return. Beckett was reading Maurice Heine carefully, as we see in a letter written on 10 January 1951:

> I am reading Heine's book at the moment. It is obviously very knowledgeable (*très calé*), with something slightly unpleasant. Good pages on 18th century atheism, how Sade goes beyond it, etc. And on the *120 Journées*. And an essay on Sade and the Roman Noir that will really upset ze Engleesh. (Beckett, 2011, 224; modified).

Maurice Heine's groundbreaking book, *Le Marquis de Sade*, contains an 'Avant-propos' to 'Dialogue between a Priest and a Dying Man', a short 'Introduction' to *The 120 Days of Sodom* and an essay on the Marquis de Sade and the 'roman noir', in which Heine tries to argue (against the evidence of most of the relevant publication dates) that Sade influenced Gothic novels in England. The book contains prefaces for the major texts, reviews and topical essays, including a review of Praz's *The Romantic Agony*. There, Heine makes the strong argument that Praz mistakes the views of Sade's characters for Sade's own philosophy

(1950, 273). In another text written as early as 1923, Heine discusses 'Sade's conception of the novel', comparing the 1791 version of *Justine* with the 1797 version, the *Nouvelle Justine*, which is much longer and much cruder. Heine's assessment is crucial if we want to understand Beckett's view of Sade; here is what he writes: 'Here and there, we encounter superb passages denouncing men's hypocrisy, the social lies, the religious myths, the shame of war or the machiavellian tricks of tyrants. The enthusiasm of the Revolution can be felt in their wordy declamations. But then orgies resume, monotonously, pitilessly and frantically' (Heine, 1950, 295). This ambivalent judgement contrasting the monotony of the pornography with the sharp political critique is shared by Beckett, as we see in a further letter of his from January 1951:

> I have finished the Heine and started translating the foreword to the *Dialogue entre un prêtre et un moribond*, a text by Sade, published incidentally in America, translation by poor old Samuel Putnam. A stirring profession of atheistic faith by Sade, brilliant things on the atheism of the Académie philosophers, a quotation from Sylvain Maréchal. I hesitated between this text and the one on Sade and the Roman Noir, equally interesting. Had a quick look at the Klossowski. Reads to me like incomparably wooly rubbish, doubt if we could find a single half-decent text in it. As for Lely, who adores Heine, who adores Sade, we must not expect much from him. Of all of them, Blanchot is by far the most intelligent. (Beckett, 2011, 224–5).

Another letter proves how deeply Beckett had been delving in Sade, for on 3 January 1952 he mentions a passage from *120 Days of Sodom*:

> And then, before we left, I happened, in the *120 Journées,* on the sun passage, inaccurately given if I remember aright. I've marked the place and will show it to you on our return. Less staggering than the first time, glimpsed in the half-light of uncut pages, but all the same, amid all those turds and sucked rectums, very welcome. (Beckett, 2011, 311).

Beckett types 'ganahuchés' (for 'sucked') instead of 'gamahuchés', which indicates a lack of familiarity with this typically Sadean term. Beckett alludes here to the moment of rest at the end of the sixth day, a day devoted to scatological games that nevertheless concludes with a peaceful Homeric simile. Beckett, who had linked Murphy and Morpheus, the god of sleep, could not but have been touched by this lyrical evocation:

> it is very probable indeed that rosy-fingered Dawn, opening the gates of Apollo's palace, would have found them lying still plunged in their excrements, rather more after the example of swine than like heroes. Needful only of rest, each lay by himself that night, and cradled in Morpheus' arms, recovered a little strength for the strenuous new day ahead. (Sade, 1987, 343)

This investment in Sade accompanied Beckett's evolution as he morphed into a French writer, from the completion of *Watt* to *Molloy*. This fascination also underpinned his temporary friendship with Bataille and his deep appreciation of the critical acumen of Blanchot.

To make sense of the fourth period, we have to skip a few years. In July 1964, when Beckett was about to go to New York to shoot *Film*, he writes: 'Got books on Sade from Mary H. for Pat' (Beckett, 2014, 607). He is alluding to the fact that he had borrowed three books from Mary Hutchinson. These include *The Revolutionary Ideas of the Marquis de Sade* by Geoffrey Gorer (1934). I highlight the publication date of Gorer's book (1934), as it is likely that Beckett read this book soon after its publication. This note shows to what extent Beckett's friendship with the Irish actor Patrick Magee, who embodied Sade in a play by Peter Weiss, extended to issues of meaning and cultural context. When Beckett noted 'Pat to play divine marquis in Weiss Marat' (604), he was aware of the political challenge posed by Weiss, and by the difficulty of performing the role of the divine Marquis as revisited in the latter's tendentious play.

Beckett came to suspect, correctly, that Patrick Magee was overwhelmed by this role. Alluding to Magee's performance at the Royal Shakespeare Company in 1965, he wrote: 'You must have your bellyful of Sade by now' (649). On 19 February 1965 Beckett attended the *Marat/Sade* play by Peter Weiss, directed by Peter Brook and played at the Aldwych Theatre. Beckett was disappointed with the performance: 'Saw Sade-Marat and Pat in Opera afterwards. Rather disappointed. Production very sloppy. ... Pat wrong I thought except in whipping scene' (658). The main critics and the audience disagreed with this negative opinion: Magee ended up winning a Tony Award in 1965 for his performance, and Peter Brook was named best director for Peter Weiss's sensational play, whose full title is *The Persecution and Assassination of Jean-Paul Marat as Performed by the Inmates of the Asylum of Charenton Under the Direction of the Marquis de Sade*. Magee completed the cycle in London in March 1965, and went on to New York, continuing to play Sade when *Marat/Sade* opened at the end of December 1965, to similarly positive critical acclaim.

The final note is sounded in a letter from 28 August 1972. Beckett returns to his frequentation of Sade and mentions a book by Guillaume Apollinaire:

> I think I know the Apollinaire Sade you mention, in a series entitled 'Les Maîtres de l'Amour' (Bibliothèque des Curieux). I once had it and find that I still have, in the same collection, his Divine Aretino in 2 vols. He must have been the initiator of the Sade boom. (Beckett, 2016, 306)

Beckett was right: Apollinaire had been the initiator of a 'Sade boom', and we will explore its inception and full flowering after World War II, beginning with Apollinaire's role in introducing Sade to a broader audience.

1 The Guides: Apollinaire, Proust and Praz

'No smoking in the torture chamber'[9]

1.1 Apollinaire

The author who made Beckett aware of the weird genius of the Marquis de Sade was Guillaume Apollinaire. We don't know when Beckett read his book on Sade, but the fact that he kept it all his life testifies to a continuous interest. Apollinaire had always been keen on erotica, and had proven himself in that genre with his *Les onze mille verges ou les amours d'un hospodar*, published in 1907, a witty title playing on the 'Eleven thousand Virgins' of Saint Ursula's fame, here transformed by a salacious double entendre into '1,100 Rods' or '1,100 Pricks'. This sly joke may have given Beckett the idea of emulating the pun when he chose *More Pricks Than Kicks* as a title. In 1909, Apollinaire published *L'Œuvre du Marquis de Sade*, a solid selection of texts accompanied by a substantial introduction, to which he added a copious bibliographical essay.[10] Apollinaire was cautious in his selection and chose texts that would look relatively innocuous, often dealing with political or moral considerations. However, he also provided a complete synopsis of the plot of the *120 Days of Sodom*, adding that the most scandalous aspect of this book derived from its licentious engravings; they came from a ten-volume illustrated version of *Justine* and *Juliette* published in 1797.

Apollinaire competently describes the first manuscript of *Justine*, a novel drafted in five notebooks. He quotes a sketch including these words: 'From beginning to end, vice triumphs, and virtue is humiliated at length', before suggesting that in the end, we see a final reversal, virtue being shown as beautiful and desirable (Apollinaire, 2014, 45). Beckett had not forgotten this lesson when he taught a class on Racine at Trinity. Leslie Daiken's lecture notes mention the name of Sade next to two famous lines from Racine's *Andromaque*:

> Je ne sais, de tout temps, quelle injuste puissance
> Laisse la paix au crime et poursuit l'innocence

---

[9] Samuel Beckett, 'Sedendo et Quiescendo' (1995, 14). This is an excerpt from *Dream of Fair to Middling Women* printed in the journal *transition* in 1932.

[10] See Apollinaire (1909, republished 2014).

(I don't know what unjust power for all times
Leave crime in peace and attacks innocence)
(qtd. in Van Hulle and Nixon, 2013, 56)

Even though Sade was known to many writers just after his death, as witnessed by Baudelaire and Flaubert, the obscenity and perversity of his works had consigned them to underground circuits of distribution. In fact, Sade was left to sexologists or denunciators of impiety, as shown by the fact that the first attempt at providing a systematic account of his work was by a German physician called Iwan Bloch, who for his books on Sade used the pseudonym Eugène Dühren. Bloch, a psychiatrist interested in promoting the then-new 'science' of sexology, discovered the manuscript of the *120 Days of Sodom*. He subsequently published it, taking the name Dühren for himself as editor, a name he would also use when he published a book entitled *Marquis de Sade* in 1899. Apollinaire quotes Dühren extensively, but unlike his German predecessor, the French poet never presents Sade as a monster or a sexual pervert whose texts offer valuable information on rare sexual aberrations. For Apollinaire, Sade is a key French writer, an important novelist and a rigorous philosopher.

Apollinaire insists on the fact that Sade was opposed to the death penalty. He portrays the Marquis as a charming man, an accomplished soldier who was a polyglot fluent in Italian, Provençal and German, an omnivorous reader who absorbed the culture of his time. Apollinaire insists on the positive role played by Sade in the Charenton mental hospital, where he would not only write plays but also direct them, and then invited the inmates to actively participate. In other words, his Sade is far from being a maniac (Apollinaire, 2014, 27). Apollinaire discusses Sade's testament (mentioned in the Introduction), that curious text in which he specified that his body should be buried in a copse at Malmaison, and his tomb concealed by sowing acorns on top of the grave (31). Apollinaire knew that this wish had not been granted. In his perspective, Sade turns into a revolutionary writer doubling as a martyr, who was punished for having insisted on the need to say everything – 'il faut tout dire' was his motto (36).[11] In fact, Beckett never rejected this positive vision of Sade as a heroic writer fighting for the right to freedom of expression, no matter what is said. Such a staunch defiance would be paralleled with Joyce's 'revolution of the word', a war waged against all literary conventions.

It is most likely that Beckett discovered the two main novels, *Justine* and *Juliette*, along with the more sulphurous *120 Days of Sodom*, in Apollinaire's anthology. Indeed, when discussing that last book, Apollinaire reverted to the

---

[11] 'La Philosophie doit tout dire' (Philosophy must say everything) is one of his favorite formulations. See Sade's *Histoire de Juliette ou Les Prospérités du Vice* (1967a, 337).

pathologizing tone that dominates in Bloch's texts: 'One finds in it a rigorously scientific classification of all the passions in their connection with the sexual instinct. Writing this, the Marquis de Sade was condensing all his new theories and created, hundred years before Krafft-Ebing, a sexual psychopathology' (Apollinaire, 2014, 51). This totalizing aspect fascinated Beckett as well. In his book, Apollinaire merely surveyed the beginning of the text and then glossed over the worst aspects, such as the frenzy of murder and horrible tortures at the end.

In his overview, Apollinaire added passages from *Zoe et ses deux acolytes* and the play *Oxtiern*. Despite inevitable limitations due to the fact that he was writing at a time when textual scholarship was barely emerging, Apollinaire offered a solid synthesis of Sade's philosophical theses while competently presenting the major works.

1.2 Mario Praz

Soon after, or at the same time, Beckett used another guide to make sense of Sade. Numerous notes taken in the *Dream Notebook* reveal that Beckett had read Mario Praz's *La carne, la morte e il diavolo nella letteratura romantica*[12] from 1930. One note, at the end of the *Notebook*, on the endpaper in fact, lists titles quoted by Praz in chapter 3 and 4 of his book:

> **Volupté:**
> Levana & our Ladies of Sorrow
> Laus Veneris
> Belle Dame Sans Merci
> Mademoiselle de Maupin
> Une Nuit de Cléopatre
> Le Roi Candaule
> Anactoria
> Lesbia Brandon
> (Beckett, 1999, 172)

These titles refer to works by Sainte-Beuve, Jean-Paul Richter, Swinburne, Keats and Gautier respectively. They take place in a systematic examination of the Marquis de Sade's influence on Romanticism and Symbolism, which culminates with Baudelaire, Flaubert and Sainte-Beuve. Chapter 3, 'Under the sign of the divine Marquis', and chapter 4, 'La Belle Dame Sans Merci', are replete with quotes from Sade. Praz's book created a sensation when it was published. No one had previously perceived those links between a darker

---

[12] I am using the second edition of Mario Praz, *La carne, la morte e il diavolo nella letteratura romantica* (Florence: Sansoni Editore, 1948 [1930]). The only modification from the edition used by Beckett is a new preface.

Enlightenment and Romanticism. Praz was the first not only to point these out but also to organize them in a consistent genealogy: for him, a diffuse Sadism had permeated the period, going from the last decade of the eighteenth century to the *fin de siècle*. Praz's book brought to Beckett an acute and exquisite literary sensibility, and it complemented what he had gleaned from Apollinaire. Maurice Heine had published *Les Infortunes de la vertu* in 1930, and the first of the three books of the *120 journées de Sodome* in 1931. Praz quotes Sade from the 1797 illustrated edition of *Justine* and *Juliette*, in ten volumes, used by Apollinaire. Most of the texts quoted come from the main diptych, *Juliette or The Infortunes of Virtue* and *Justine or The Prosperities of Vice*.

As we saw, Beckett found it expedient that Praz should leave Sade's abundant quotes in the original French, which allowed him to provide textual examples of the vivacity of the style. It is clear that Beckett read these pages attentively. Praz offers a more literary view of Sade's world, even if one can say that the picture he presents is partially distorted. In his analyses, Praz did not follow an exact historical progression. He began with readings of Poe translated by Baudelaire, for Baudelaire functioned as his main guide in his historical reconstruction. Indeed, Baudelaire had written: 'Il faut toujours en revenir à Sade, c'est-à-dire à l'homme naturel, pour expliquer le mal' ('One should always go back to Sade, that is to natural man, in order to explain evil'; Praz, 1948, 152). Baudelaire had also declared: 'En réalité, le satanisme a gagné. Satan s'est fait ingénu. Le mal se connaissant était moins affreux et plus près de la guérison que le mal s'ignorant. G. Sand inférieure à Sade' ('In reality, satanism has won. Satan has become a naïve. Evil knowing itself was less awful, closer to healing, than an evil unaware of itself. G. Sand inferior to Sade'; 105). Baudelaire's jaundiced critique of one of the best-known female novelists of the nineteenth century misled Praz, making him believe that Sade manifested a 'Satanist' disposition.

However, when Praz compared Sade's 'Thérèse philosophe' with Jean-Jacques Rousseau ('Thus Thérèse, anticipating Rousseau...') (Praz, 1948, 101), he remained on safer ground. Praz was one of the first critics to stress the fairly obvious view that Sade systematically inverted Rousseau's optimism. Rousseau thought that human beings, essentially good, had been corrupted by society. Sade saw humans as fundamentally evil, wicked or bestial. Anticipating Nietzsche's insights, he presents the whole of society as founded on desperate attempts by morality to conceal this cynical truth. If there were a God (although this is not the case), it could only be an evil God, a vindictive and unjust Creator, as Juliette thinks and as Praz notes (106). A passage from *Justine* insists on the fact that murder is the rule in the state of nature. Nature evinces countless instances of senseless slaughter. Its only law is that of utter destruction, not that of the propagation of the species (Praz, 1948, 106). In four pages, Praz gives eleven eloquent quotes from *Justine* and *Juliette* that confirm this logic.

Looking at the text closely, Praz then notices a crucial contradiction: if on the one hand, Sade endorses a naturalism that teaches human beings to accept their fates as either predators or victims – better be a predator and follow our criminal instincts, then! – on the other hand, his Libertines attack Nature as well. Sade's thesis is reiterated in two parallel novels, *Justine* and *Juliette*: with Juliette, vice triumphs; with Justine, virtue is punished. Sade multiplies theories about why murder should be accepted and even accomplished remorselessly, for in the end, there is nothing but the redistribution of atoms recombined by natural forces. Thus there is no evil if one decides to follow one's innate cruelty (Praz, 1948, 108). This thesis ends up clashing with a more dramatic, sensualist and contrarian view, for according to Sade acts of utter destruction should give pleasure. In fact, infamy seduces much more than virtuous restraint.

Sade keeps praising excessive enjoyment, the true ecstasy of the Libertines, many of whom are women; an enjoyment mostly experienced when inflicting pain on others, the root of the active algolagnia Sade's name has been identified with. If this seems 'unnatural', this derives from the fact that it is Nature that should be outraged. Sade reveals himself to be not a cynic but an enthusiast whose ecstasies hinge on a sense of hubris. In *Justine*, a Libertine exclaims:

> It is nature I would like to outrage. I would like to perturb its plans, block its progression, halt the revolution of the stars, upset the globes floating in space, destroy what serves it, protect what harms it, shore up what irritates it, in a word insult it in all its works. (qtd. in Praz, 1948, 109)

Praz concludes humorously that if one wanted most to go against the grain of nature, the best way would be to return to virtue (109)!

What Sade requires, then, in spite of his contradictions (although we should note that these speeches are given by different characters whose ideologies are at variance), is the right or even the duty to say everything; this claim is in itself revolutionary. It attacks conventional morality by inverting the foundations of the metaphysics of morals in a striking anticipation of Nietzsche. Praz notes that the Introduction to *Justine* extends the notion of the 'soul': 'Quant aux tableaux cyniques, nous croyons, avec l'auteur, que toutes les situations possibles de l'âme étant à la disposition du romancier, il n'en est aucune dont il n'ait la permission de faire usage' ('As for cynical tableaux, we believe with the author that all the possible situations of the soul being available to a novelist, there is none that he would not be allowed to use'; 109). By foregrounding this theme, Praz announces Maurice Blanchot's main contention. For Blanchot, Sade's Reason is not the faculty praised by the Enlightenment, because it is a delirious Reason. Its teeming contradictions vouch for this delirium. However, because such an 'Unreason' struggles to find an expression, because it aims at expressing the inexpressible more than the obscene or the purely transgressive, the consequences are positive: Sade pushes the art of the novel further and opens up new spaces for writing.

Praz examines the numerous writers who have tried to refute Sade in vain, like Restif de la Bretonne with his *Anti-Justine, ou les Délices de l'amour* (1798), or those who were influenced by him more or less covertly. He focuses on Swinburne as the most Sadean British poet. Although Sade may owe a lot to Gothic novels, Swinburne goes further, as his impact on Baudelaire proves. Baudelaire's genius was to combine Poe's 'imp of the perverse' with a satanic enjoyment of transgression in the matter of love – this view by Praz provided a key insight for the younger Beckett. Baudelaire noted that 'love's unique and supreme pleasure lies in the certainty of accomplishing something *evil*' (qtd. in Praz, 1948, 154). Reviewing Jules Janin, Thomas de Quincey and P. J. Toulet, Praz unearths sadism in Flaubert, from the first *Sentimental Education* to *The Temptation of Saint Anthony*. Praz notes with relish that when Isidore Ducasse presented a renewal of Sadean Gothicism in the *Chants de Maldoror*, it was a direct offshoot of Baudelaire's satanism. A long footnote at the end of chapter 3 links the sadistic fantasies of Lautréamont to the Surrealism of Breton and Soupault.

Indeed, in the 1930s, one could not ignore that Sade had been enlisted among the precursors of Surrealism. The first manifesto of Surrealism defined Sade with a quasi-tautology: 'Sade is Surrealist in Sadism' (Breton, 1969, 26). Breton's epigram might surprise his readers, especially those who remember that he had been trained as a psychiatrist. The sentence betrays a certain embarrassment facing what Beckett later called 'sadism pure and simple'; the complex relation between 'sadism' in general as a rather common perversion, and the literary Sadism of the Marquis de Sade. Against Breton's equivocation, Georges Bataille would decide to appeal to a truly materialist Sade; this came as he was breaking with Breton, when Sade was the main example of a 'base materialism' that he felt was lacking in Breton. And then Breton's second Surrealist manifesto from 1930 responded to Bataille by accusing him of being an 'anti-dialectical' materialist (183). The violence of this rejoinder had been triggered by Bataille's own violence. Breton rejected the apocryphal vignette in which Bataille presented Sade locked up at Charenton, ordering a bunch of beautiful roses only to dip then into liquid manure. Although that gesture might be acceptable when coming from a literary martyr who had spent twenty-seven years of his life in prison, it could not be tolerated when coming from a 'staid librarian', as Breton called Bataille (186). This quarrel between two versions of Surrealism in which the role of Sade became a veritable symptom has been abundantly discussed (see Trahan, 2017). Beckett was spared the quandary of having to choose between Bataille and Breton, a quandary that Salvador Dalí would later have to face, for when he was associated with the neo-Surrealist magazine *transition*, the name of Sade rarely appeared. However, because of his friendship with Georges Duthuit, Beckett's allegiance moved clearly to the side of Bataille after the war (see Albright, 2003, 1–27; Friedman, 2018).

Far from that fray, keeping an ironical distance, Praz extolled Baudelaire, preferring him to Breton or Lautréamont as a guide. Baudelaire is the most fecund influence when he sketches his vast fresco of decadence; indeed, 'Byzantium', the last chapter of his book, culminates with a survey of European decadence in which Baudelaire, Pater and Swinburne are relayed by Schopenhauer, Nietzsche and Wagner. What stands out is Baudelaire's version of sadism, rewritten and interpreted by Praz: this sadism is defined as a dialectical relation, for as Praz reiterates, the French poet presents the roles of victim and tormentor as exchangeable, quoting: 'It might be sweet to be alternatively victim and torturer' (qtd. in Praz, 1948, 155). Praz surveys the numerous poems in *Flowers of Evil* in which the poet presents himself as a vampire. This literary sadism was refined and developed by Swinburne, as in the novel quoted earlier, *Lesbia Brandon*.

Praz sums up *Lesbia Brandon* cogently when he says that it combines incest, lesbianism and hermaphroditism. At some point, the male hero Denham asks the woman he is infatuated with to walk all over his body:

> 'I wish you would kill me some day; it would be so jolly to feel you killing me. Not like it? Shouldn't I! You just hurt me and see.' She pinched him so sharply that he laughed and panted with pleasure. 'I should like being swished even I think, if you were to complain of me or if I knew you liked it.' (qtd. in Praz, 1948, 236)

The temptation of passive algolagnia was transmitted to the heirs of Baudelaire's Héautontimorouménos, the artist who punishes himself, saying:

> Je suis la plaie et le couteau!
> Je suis le soufflet et la joue!
> Je suis les membres et la roue,
> Et la victime et le bourreau!
>
> (I am the wound and the knife!
> I am the slap and the face!
> I am the limbs and the wheel,
> and the victim and the executioner!)
>   (qtd. in Praz, 1948, 236)

Accordingly, this defines the contours of the first sadism invoked by Beckett, the sadism that we find in *Dream*, a literary sadism combining satanism with a principle of reversibility between active and passive roles.

A sign of this conjunction appears in Beckett's first published short story, 'Assumption' (Beckett, 1995a, 3–7). Its publication accompanied his essay on Joyce ('Dante ... Bruno. Vico . . Joyce') in *transition* 16/17. As Céline Mansanti has pointed out, the style of Beckett's story clashes with that deployed by the other avant-gardist experimenters. The story sounds more decadent, in fact; indeed, it could have been written by Swinburne (188–9). In this early text, Beckett plays on stereotypes inherited from late Romanticism and German expressionism, the topos of intense sexual passion causing the death of one of the partners. Poe would treat it in a Gothic manner, Robert Browning as an interior monologue with 'Porphyria's Lover' (1836) and Oskar Kokoschka as an expressionist drama in *Mörder, Hoffnung der Frauen* (1909). In Beckett's story, the male partner dies at the end, apparently swept away by the storm released by the orgasmic scream of the allegorical woman. Under the cover of the Christian notion of 'assumption', meaning 'being taken to the skies', Beckett literalizes the concept of a 'little death' brought about by orgasmic sex, to which he adds a touch of satanism: 'Until at last, for the first time, he was unconditioned by the Satanic dimensional Trinity, he was released, achieved, the blue flower, Vega, GOD ... ' (Beckett, 1995a, 6). The female partner is called 'the Woman', a generic force intervening as the arch destroyer. Moreover, the young man is a willing victim, an accomplice in the sexual dissolution leading to his demise. As in many texts of Sade, the orgasmic uplift is presented as a sort of epileptic seizure thanks to which sex and death finally merge.

A passage of *Dream* proves that Beckett's reading of Praz generated more dialectical couples. Following Praz's thesis about Sade, Beckett works with a double dichotomy: he contrasts Justine and Juliette first, then sadism and masochism. This appears when Belacqua returns to Paris, where his friends expect him. He is uncertain about continuing his relationship with the Smeraldina, in whom one recognizes his cousin Peggy, who is too passionate and sentimental; next to his gay French friend whose conversation inspires him more than the Smeraldina's prattle, he is also tempted sexually by the Syracusa (a barely concealed Lucia Joyce, then living in Paris):

> That was the modus vivendi, poised between God and the Devil, Justine and
> Juliette, at the dead point, in a tranquil living at the neutral point, a living dead
> to love-God and love-Devil, poised without love above the fact of the royal
> flux westering headlong. .... I can only know the real poise at the crest of the
> relation rooted in the unreal postulates, God-Devil, Masoch-Sade (he might

have spared us that hoary old binary), Me-You, One-minus One. (Beckett,
1992, 27–8)

This passage does not reflect a deep understanding of Sade's philosophy,
although his name is dropped strategically in the context of sexual tension,
evincing a certain hesitation between these very opposites. If Belacqua's attitude leans towards masochistic passivity, he cannot help being sadistic in the
pain he inflicts on his young women. Like Swinburne, he has a physical dread of
simple and uncomplicated sexual rapports.

This sadomasochism betrays a certain misogyny, which is a recurrent feature
of *Dream*. Misogyny expands and rebounds when we meet satirical portraits,
evocations of typical female Dublin types like the Frica. Her particular attitude
is summed up by the fact that she carries a volume by Sade:

> In she lands singing Havelock Ellis in a deep voice, itching manifestly to
> work that which is not seemly. If only she could be bound and beaten and
> burnt, but not quick. Or, failing that, brayed gently in a mortar. Open her
> concave breast as on a lectern lies Portigliotti's *Penumbre Claustrali* bound in
> tawed caul. In her talons earnestly she clutches Sade's *Hundred Days* and the
> *Anterotica* of Aliosha G. Brignole-Sale, unopened, bound in shagreened caul.
> (Beckett, 1992, 179)

An anachronism should make us pause: at the time the action is supposed to take
place, there existed no English translation of the *120 Days of Sodom*. Besides,
here the number of days has been rounded off to one hundred. On top of that, it is
unlikely that Beckett ever looked up Brignole-Sale's works. The seventeenth-
century ambassador, who authored both erotic books and religious treatises, had
become a Jesuit after the death of his wife. Beckett owes this learned reference
to Praz, who knew about him from *Penombre Claustrali* by G. Portigliotti,
a book describing Brignole-Sale's perverse habits (Praz, 1948, 54 n27). A note
in the *Dream Notebook* identifies him as a 'champion flagellator' (Beckett,
1999, 36). Whatever his masochistic dispositions may have been, Brignole-Sale
would never have been called Aliosha, like one of the Karamazov brothers.

The Frica sends us to Mary Manning, whose mother similarly kept an open
literary salon. Their intense erotic adventure would have to wait until the
summer of 1936, when Beckett and Mary Manning Howe engaged in
a passionate but short-lived affair. She had to be rushed to Boston in order to
avoid a scandal; some believed her elder daughter, the poet Susan Howe, to be
Beckett's daughter. Here again, the quoted books derive from Praz.
Such second-hand work betrays its limits: Beckett did not remember the exact
number of days. When he rewrote that passage for *More Pricks Than Kicks*, he
changed 100 to the correct 120. Beckett makes fun of the predatory sexuality of

the young liberated ladies in Dublin. The Frica resembles a Proustian character, for she appears like a Madame Verdurin of eroticism.

1.3 Proust

The first 'sadistic' scene in Proust's *Recherche* surprises readers as much as it shocks the young narrator, but it may not be for the same reasons. What Proust's synopsis calls a 'scene of sadism at Montjouvain' does not fit our usual understanding of what sadism entails; we are privy to a scene of moral torture enacted by two lesbian lovers. Mlle Vinteuil is justifiably in mourning because her father, a composer who doted on her, has just died. She deliberately pulls out her father's portrait as her lover arrives. They decide to leave the windows open, daring any voyeur, like the narrator, to keep on looking. After some amorous romps, Mlle Vinteuil spits on her father's portrait. The narrator flees in horror, not without having meditated on the lesson in perversity. It is a lesson in paradox, for he surmises that Mlle Vinteuil is pure at heart yet feels the need for transgression. She needs to stage ritual profanations of what she loves most, the memory of her dead father, when she is with her lover. Proust's considerations generalize her attitude:

> A sadist of her sort is an artist of evil, something that an entirely bad creature could not be, for then evil would not be exterior to her, it would seem to her quite natural, would not even be distinguishable from hers; and as for virtue, memory of the dead, and filial tenderness, since she would not be devoutly attached to them she would take no sacrilegious pleasure in profaning them. Sadists of Mlle. Vinteuil's kind are creatures so purely sentimental, so naturally virtuous, that even sensual pleasure seems to them as something bad, the privilege of the wicked. And when they allow themselves to yield to it for a moment, they are trying to step into the skin of the wicked and to make their partner do so as well, so as to have the illusion for a moment, of escaping from their scrupulous and tender soul into the inhuman world of pleasure. (Proust, 2002, 167–8)

Soon the narrator discovers that this alleged 'sadism' occurs frequently. It consists less in enjoying the pain of other people than in a complex system that distributes tortures and felicities evenly. It is in this context that Beckett places side by side Dante and Proust, in an attempt to query the role pain plays in the Dantean model of the *Inferno*. There is no need to belabour the point: Beckett's book on Proust is steeped in the philosophy of Schopenhauer. As *The World as Will and Representation* explains, Dante's Hell is merely a vision of this world: 'For whence did Dante get the material for his hell, if not from the actual world of ours?' (Schopenhauer, 1969, I: 325). Schopenhauer analyses the temptation of rejecting the source of pain in the world, which is the temptation of mortification and self-torture: the subject will then tend to 'resort to fasting, and even to self-castigation and self-torture, in order that, by constant privation and suffering, he may more and more break down and kill the will that he recognizes and abhors as the source of his own suffering existence and the world's' (382). Close to the end of the book, Schopenhauer discusses quietism and Buddhism, which he equates with radical asceticism and self-torture (607), all these being dangerous forms of the denial of the will. If Beckett will later explore the 'blessedness of will-less perception', as Schopenhauer puts it (198), in novels such as *Murphy*, then his early work is more concerned with the issue of pain and expiation facing divine justice.

We know how Dante's sinners expiate their sins in a logic of retribution founded upon a sort of divine sadism. Beckett's poem 'Text 3' explores the interaction of pain, pity and divine justice. It begins with the first word spoken to Virgil by Dante the character, *Miserere*, which is not an Italian word but a Latin prayer: '*Miserere* di me' ('Have pity on me'; *Inferno*, I, 65). We glimpse Dante's synthetic language, but here it is not Joyce who is compared with Dante, as in Beckett's famous essay, but Proust, for a meditation on the juxtaposition of goodness and sadism:

> Proust's cook is in the study,
> she is grieving in a general way for the abstract intestine,
> she is so engrossed that she does not hear the screams of her assistant,
> a sloven she,
> and the dying spit of a Paduan Virtue,
> for alas she has stripped her last asparagus,
> now she is smashed on delivery.
> She rises,
> her heart is full of murder and tears,
> she hunts down the pullet with oaths,
> fiercely she tears his little head off.

(Beckett, 2012, 38)

Proust highlights the mixture of cruelty and compassion that marks all his characters. In this case, the character is Françoise's assistant, a kitchen maid both sickly and pregnant. Françoise tortures her morally and mercilessly until the woman leaves. Thus the narrator and his family are surprised to be served asparagus at all their meals: Françoise knows that the kitchen maid is prone to asthma attacks when peeling it (Proust, 2002, 127). Later, the maid screams in pain during her difficult delivery; Françoise fetches a book describing her ailment; she does not return to help the poor woman, but is later discovered engrossed in the book, now full of compassion for those who suffer similar pains. She exclaims: 'Oh dear, Holy Virgin, is it possible that the good Lord would want a wretched human creature to suffer so?'(125).

This segues to the later moment when the narrator surprises Françoise in the kitchen; deprived of her usual helper, she must kill a recalcitrant chicken herself. Furious, she cries out repeatedly: 'Vile Creature!' ('Sale bête!') (124). Even when the animal is beheaded and its blood collected, the oath is repeated. Shocked, the narrator first wants to have her dismissed, but then reflects that without her, he would be deprived of sublime food at lunch and dinner. This makes him pardon her. Beckett's poem insists on Françoise's cruelty, whereas Proust made room for moral laxity given the 'cowardly calculations' (125) that cannot but arise in similar circumstances.[13] Beckett has followed Proust in his subtle meditations on affective ambivalence, and in his awareness that a certain sadism tinges the most ethical attitudes.

Later scenes of sadism in Proust's novel appear more conventional, but their lesson for the narrator is no less paradoxical; one takes place during the war, when Paris is bombed by German airplanes and is deserted, its dark streets taking on the appearance of a biblical Sodom. The older Baron Charlus is seen by the narrator being flogged in Jupien's male brothel. Once more occupying a voyeuristic role, the narrator sees Charlus repeatedly whipped by a young man who pretends to be a murderer. Praz had quoted Proust as stating that nothing is more limited than pleasure and vice (107). Not resisting the pun, Praz sees those vicious subjects moving in vicious circles, which develops Proust's main idea and connects it with Dante's.

Sadism is mentioned several times in *Time Regained*. Proust's sadists are at bottom 'pure souls' inhabited by a perverse but universal thirst for evil. Beckett was right to conclude that there was no moral sense in Proust. Writing the first English monograph on Proust in 1931, Beckett noticed an absence of moral sense in *La Recherche*: 'Proust is completely detached from all moral considerations. There is no right and wrong in Proust nor in his world' (Beckett, 1970, 66). The evocation of several 'Albertines' multiplies the narrator's fickle lover into contradictory figures evolving 'into a *plastic* and moral multiplicity' (47; emphasis in original). Contradictions in her being evince 'a multiplicity in depth, a turmoil of objective and immanent contradictions over which the subject has no control' (47). What the narrator loves in the elusive but constantly lying Albertine is not her disappointing body or her trite mind, for both soon bore him, but the way her capacity for infinite otherness generates both endless pain and absolute *jouissance*.

---

[13] See also Marcel Proust, *A la recherche du temps perdu* (1987, I: 120).

2 From *Murphy* to *Watt*: Knotting Pathology and Theology

Let us note the coincidence of the dates: Beckett was asked to translate Sade at the time he was revising and correcting the proofs for *Murphy*, just after he had been stabbed in a Paris street at night, coming very close to dying. As we saw, Kahane had made the offer for the Sade translation in February, just after Beckett had returned the proofs for *Murphy* in January 1938. *Murphy* was published in March 1938. If sadism plays a minor role in *Murphy*, it is nevertheless present. Sadism is associated with the new scene offered by the asylum, in connection with one character whose name returns in subsequent texts (a clown's name in fact), Bom, the top male nurse: 'Bom was what is vulgarly called a sadist and encouraged what is vulgarly called sadism in his assistants' (Beckett, 1957, 238). This 'vulgar' sadism is described in terms of energy: 'If during the day this energy could not be discharged with any great freedom even on those patients who submitted to it as part and parcel of the therapeutic voodoo, with still less freedom could it be discharged on those who regarded it as *hors d'oeuvre*' (238). It might be anachronistic to enlist Beckett in an antipsychiatric critique of an institution like the hospital. There is nevertheless a close scrutiny of the abuses of medical power in the context of mental health. Typically, those inmates who refuse harsh treatments are called 'uncooperative' or 'resistive' (both in quotation marks in the text), while the treatment they receive is not much better than voodoo or sorcery. If they resist, they are likely to 'get hell at night' (238).

After this general evocation of a quasi-Dantean setting, the narrative shows how institutional sadism clashes with Murphy's selfless devotion, his empathy with mental patients in the mental hospital being his main quality. However, the torturing Bim and Bom cannot be taken too seriously, for their names echo those of well-known Russian clowns. Ivan Radunsky was Bim, and a number of other entertainers played several 'Boms'. Although they were popular in Russia before and after World War I, they were often censored for their sallies. The duo of Bim and Bom was the most popular entertainment in Civil War Moscow. Beckett uses this Russian reference to make fun of the institution's repressive policies. The clowns reappear in *What Where*, as we will see, following the logic of what Bruce Nauman called 'clown torture' in his infamous 1987 videos.[14] In chapter 9 of *Murphy*, we meet the personnel of the mental hospital, notable for the curious presence of several clown-like figures among them. They have

---

[14] Bruce Nauman, *Clown Torture* (1987), four tapes with many repeats, including the scenes, 'Clown Taking a Shit', 'Clown With a Goldfish', 'Clown With Water Bucket', 'Pete and Repeat', and 'No, No, No, No (Walter)'; Reel B: 'Clown With Goldfish', 'Clown With Water Bucket'. See www.artic.edu › artworks › clown-torture.

funny names like Bim (Clinch), whose 'nepotism' leads him to hire seven male relations including Bom and Bum (Beckett, 1957, 166). Then we encounter Tom and Tim (169). The people inhabiting the MMM fall into two categories: a fierce 'battle' rages 'between the psychotic and psychiatric points of view' (165).

By calling Bom's sadism 'vulgar', Beckett implies that it has little to do with Sade's writings, although, as we will see, he will be interested by the role Sade played in the prefiguration of modern mental hospitals when he was obliged to live in the Charenton clinic. Halfway between Bom's vulgar sadism and Murphy's attentive care for the inmates, there is Mr Endon, the psychotic patient with whom Murphy will somehow identify. After their fateful game of chess, we discover that Endon is not immured in his psychosis to the point that he cannot exert his own sadism: we learn that he kept switching the light on and off in the hypomanic's cell, who then 'bounced off the walls like a bluebottle in a jar' (247).

Between *Murphy*'s padded cells, happy lunatics and less fortunate hypomanics and the curious institution in which Watt and Sam meet in the third chapter of *Watt*, there are minor differences in style and kind. The chapter begins abruptly when we learn that Watt had been 'transferred to another pavilion', which restricts the frequency of his conversations with Sam (Beckett, 1953, 151). Sam, who has suddenly emerged as the narrator, is another inhabitant of the 'mansions' they are given, and both avoid the 'other scum, cluttering up the passageways, the hallways, grossly loud, blatantly morose' (152). They have their 'attendants', but what is more disquieting is that not only are their rooms said to be windowless (152), but that the gardens to which they are allowed access are surrounded with barbed wire (156) and that their fences are so sharp that people passing along them might be 'impaled' and 'bleed to death' (157). Obviously, the mental asylum has surreptitiously turned into a death camp, although these topographical precisions soon evaporate, to let the characters launch endless conversations.

If Murphy was shown to fail in his wish to be like Spinoza's God, a God whose infinite love is directed to himself in *amor intellectualis* (Beckett, 1957, 107), as much as in his attempt at approximating Endon's self-sufficiency, in *Watt*, the question of a godlike self-love takes a different turn. *Watt* splices together a philosophical meditation on the uses of Reason, deriving from Beckett's reading of Kant, with a world view predicated on Dante and Sade.

Watt, begun in Paris during the war, was mostly written between 1942 and 1945 when Beckett was hiding from the Gestapo in Roussillon. Was Beckett aware of the curious fact that this beautiful village in the Vaucluse region of Southern France was within sight of the neighbouring village of La Coste, which was once the location of the Marquis de Sade's castle, between the lovely villages of Ménerbes and Bonnieux? Indeed, at that time, the castle was mostly in ruins, but was still visible from the ridge on top of Roussillon when one faced south, looking towards the slightly higher Lubéron mountains. What would Beckett have thought of this proximity, a mere five miles away as the crow flies, at a time when history seemed to show a renewal of sadism with all its attendant torture chambers, and when, as Pasolini demonstrated in *Salò*, the terrifying film adaptation of *The 120 Days of Sodom*, Sade's fantasies had perhaps come back to haunt humanity like a living nightmare?

One may pose the question knowing that Beckett took to Sade's works for a variety of reasons. When he was about to translate *The 120 Days of Sodom*, he had been struck by 'a kind of metaphysical ecstasy' and compared Sade's composition with the rigorous organization of Dante's universe (Beckett, 2009, 607). Beckett saw the 'surface obscenity' as not pornographic. Indeed, Sade very systematically tries to show everything, including pure obscenity, but his practice of textual and sexual excess never attempts to seduce the reader with erotic images. What is most striking is that he consistently tries to convince his readers of his sanity by using reason.

This preamble is necessary to understand how sadism operates in *Watt*. A good place to examine it would be the passage of the third chapter when we are told of one of Sam's and Watt's favourite pastimes during their conversations. One of these is a little game they have invented with rats:

> But our particular friends were the rats, that dwelt by the stream. They were long and black. We brought them tidbits from our ordinary as rinds of cheese, and morsels of gristle, and we brought them also birds' eggs, and frogs, and fledglings. Sensible of these attentions, they would come flocking round us at our approach, with every sign of confidence and affection, and glide up our trouserlegs, and hang upon our breasts. And then we would sit down in the midst of them, and give them to eat, out of our hands, of a nice fat frog, or a baby thrush. Or seizing suddenly a plump young rat, resting in our bosom after its repast, we would feed it to its mother, or its father, or its sister, or to some less fortunate relative.
>
> It was on these occasions, we agreed, after an exchange of views, that we came nearest to God. (Beckett, 1953, 155–56)

We can recognize here the usual features of a Sadean cruelty whose perversity entails a reversal of pastoral Rousseauism. Watt and Sam had been presented frolicking in meadows, seemingly enjoying the charms of Mother Nature. Taking the example of the sudden rages that seize Sade's heroes, Watt and Sam destroy the confidence they have built with these animals and show that the fundamental law of Nature is mutual aggression and murder. The object of the transgressive gesture is not chosen at random, for it aims at motherhood and fatherhood, thereby subverting the notion of the family as the site of mutual respect and morality. Sam's and Watt's gesture shifts vertiginously from goodness for animals to vicious cruelty, surprising the poor creatures who had believed in their benevolence. Like Sade's talkative torturers, the two friends 'reason' upon their gesture, thus elaborating a whole discourse leading to the heights of an anti-theology, for it seems that they aspire to emulate an absolutely evil God.

This is the picture of Sade that had been elaborated in the 1930s by a key writer mentioned by Beckett, Pierre Klossowski. In his early essay 'Elements for a Psychoanalytic Study of Marquis de Sade', Klossowski detailed the hatred of the mother in Sade, his rejection of fecundity leading him to praise sodomy and incest. For Klossowski, the main Sadean fantasy is to see the father deflower his own daughter and incite her to torture and murder her mother (2001, 39). Klossowski sees this destruction of the conventional family as founded on an appeal to an evil God, a principle that he calls the 'Supreme Being in Cruelty' ('Être suprême en méchanceté'; 43, 55). One Libertine at least, Saint-Fond, appeals to this evil god in *Juliette*. According to Saint-Fond's inverted theology, this sinister God can only rejoice when he sees evil spreading in the world: indeed, he is 'a very vindictive being, very barbarous, very wicked, very unjust, very cruel' (Sade, 1967a, 397).

Without going to such extremities, Beckett mentioned his own mother's imperious nature in at least one letter from October 1937, which establishes a link between his mother's overbearing presence and his sense of being tortured by her. Only after his psychoanalysis with Bion could Beckett confess this to MacGreevy:

> I am what her savage loving has made me, and it is good that one of us should accept that finally. As it has been all this time, she wanting me to behave in a way agreeable to her in her October of analphabetic gentility, or to her friends ditto, or to the business code of father idealized – dehumanised – . . . – the grotesque can go no further. It is like after a long forenoon of the thumb screws being commanded by the bourreau to play his favorite song without words with feeling. (Beckett, 2009, 552)

Of course, Beckett never went as far as Sade did in *Philosophy in the Bedroom*, in which we see the mother defiled, raped and humiliated when she comes to 'save' her daughter from the Libertines, who are instructing her in the arts of debauchery. Sade's Libertines have such a hatred of religion that in *The 120 Days of Sodom* the most severely punished violation is the mention of God. When Sam and Watt act like a perverse God with rats, they choose these lowly creatures because they reject any consensus about being 'human'. Rats traverse the layers of pseudo-humanity that we think we inhabit, from a voracious greed for godlike transcendence to the frenzied panic of animals caught up in the midst of death throes, as Hugo von Hofmannsthal's famous 'Letter of Lord Chandos' showed. It is in the tension between an unnamable humanity and its worst perversions that something like a law, the imperative of saying upon which Beckett's decision to write rests, can be thought out.

Given its insistence on the issue of the conditions of possibility and impossibility, *Watt* has been described as deploying a Kantian philosophy. This is P. J. Murphy's convincingly argued thesis in 'Beckett and the Philosophers', where he states: 'Watt is a Kantian novel' (1994, 229). One might qualify this by adding that *Watt* is as Kantian as it is Sadean, for the two 'laws' can be paralleled. The link between Kant and Sade had been perceived by Sade's immediate contemporaries, as Michel Delon, the editor of the first volume of Sade in the prestigious Pléiade series, observes. Delon quotes an essay from a revolutionary publication:

> If the pleasure given to me by the exercise of virtue is of the same nature as my physical enjoyment [*jouissances physiques*], if the approbation of my conscience is only a pleasant trickling of my nerves, what will I say to those who prefer one pleasure to another? What will I say to the brigand and the thief who take pleasure in their crimes, if it is not just that they should be careful not to be caught and punished? And, since we have to show in its most horrible light this awful system, what will its devotees reply to the author of *Justine*? Will they not have to agree that he is the most logical among those they have adopted? If one posits as principle that everything depends upon sensation, there will be no difference between a hero who saves his fatherland and a monster wallowing in mud and blood. (Delon, 1990, 24)[15]

The parallel between Kant and Sade had been made by Simone de Beauvoir as well; she saw a similar puritan root in their philosophies. In a groundbreaking 1951 essay, tellingly entitled 'Must We Burn Sade?', an essay that Beckett must have read, de Beauvoir pointed out similarities between Sade's philosophy of excess and Kant's notion of freedom: 'With a severity similar to Kant's, and which has its source in the same puritan tradition, Sade conceives the free act only as an act free of all feeling. If it were to obey emotional motives, it would make us Nature's slaves again and not autonomous subjects' (qtd. in Sade, 1987, 55).[16] Sade would invert Kant's philosophy ironically: he disturbs and provokes it by embodying revolutionary terror in literature, and makes philosophy play the role of an evil demon, a Cartesian *malin génie* whose critique of

---

[15] In the *Bibliothèque française*, Fructidor an IX (September 1801).

[16] First published under that title in *Les Temps modernes* (no. 74, December 1951), and republished in a collection of essays entitled *Privilèges* (1955).

morality becomes hyperbolical. He gives universal reason the task of proclaiming atheism, founding materialism on a rejection of morality, and offering the most extreme debauch a social sanction.

A textual confirmation of the conflation of Sade and Kant is given in the 'Addenda' inserted at the end of *Watt*, for they look very much like the Addenda that Sade added at the end of *The 120 Days of Sodom*. In a series of frenzied afterthoughts, Sade appended quite a few 'Supplementary Tortures', one of which would reappear in Freud's case of obsessional neurosis, the famous 'Ratman', obsessed by the story of a Chinese torture involving a rat, the anus and a burning bowl. The torture has been feminized, both for the agent and the victim, in Sade's version: 'By means of a hollow tube, a mouse is introduced into her cunt, the tube is withdrawn, the cunt sewn up, and the animal unable to get out, devours the entrails' (1987, 673). On the whole, *Watt*'s Addenda make fun of all symbolical or allegorical interpretations, all the while referring to Kant by quoting '*das fruchtbare Bathos der Erfahrung*' ('the fruitful bathos of experience'; Beckett, 1953, 253).

This phrase comes from *Prolegomena to Any Future Metaphysics*, in which Kant attacks a reviewer who had misunderstood his first Critique. Bathos means literally 'low place', and thus points to the locus of the earth, as in the 'base materialism' about which Bataille was endlessly talking in the 1930s. In the novel, Knott calls up Kant, if the moral law formalizes what one 'can't do'. On the whole, Beckett's project is comparable to what Adorno and Horkheimer accomplish in *Dialectic of Enlightenment*, a book coincidentally written at the same time as *Watt* by these two exiles from Nazi Germany. Like the refugees from the Frankfurt school, Beckett aims at a radical questioning of the 'madness of Reason', as he explained in an interview with Michael Haerdter:

> The crisis started with the end of the 17th century, after Galileo. The 18th century has been called the century of reason, *le siècle de la Raison*. I've never understood that; they're all mad, *ils sont tous fous, ils déraisonnent!* They give reason a responsibility which it simply can't bear, it's too weak. The Encyclopedists wanted to know everything ... But that direct relation between the self and – as the Italians say – *lo scibile*, the knowable, was already broken. (qtd. in McMillan and Fehsenfeld, 1988, 231)

The parallel between Kant and Sade sends us back to a law that transcends any human concerns, which is the thesis developed by Max Horkheimer in chapter 2 of *The Dialectic of Enlightenment*. While Horkheimer drafted the chapter on Kant and Sade, both Adorno and Horkheimer accuse Kantian 'pure Reason' of being sadistic in essence. They see the culmination of the Enlightenment's reverence for 'light' in a cult of Reason that contains the seeds of a calculating rationality, which will end up ushering a totalitarian order linked with capitalism. Its exact equivalent is the systematic mechanization of pleasures in Sade's perverse utopias. The *Critique of Practical Reason* stresses the autonomy and self-determination of the moral subject, and defines thereby the pure form of ethical action. In Kant, the philosophy of Enlightenment meets global capitalism with a vengeance: any human concern has to be ruled out; what matters is merely the conformity of Reason with its own laws, a Reason that must then appear abstract and devoid of any object.

If human affects are pushed away from an independent and all-powerful Reason, the criminal Juliette is more logical than Kant; she draws the conclusions that Kant avoids: the bourgeois order of society justifies crime, provided crime be regulated by a rationality that controls all activities and pleasures. The Sadean 'apathy' often mentioned by Blanchot functions like an equivalent of Kantian 'disinterestedness'. As Horkheimer and Adorno write:

> 'Apathy (considered as strength) is a necessary presupposition of virtue', writes Kant, distinguishing, not unlike Sade, between this 'moral apathy' and insensibility in the sense of indifference to sensory stimulation. . . . Juliette's friend Clairwil makes exactly the same observation with regard to vice. 'My soul is hardened, and I am far from preferring sensibility to the happy indifference I now enjoy.' (2002, 75)

As the two philosophers explain, 'apathy' arose at a turning point in the evolution of the bourgeoisie. This complex virtue is needed to let the 'brutal efficiency' of the bourgeoisie conquer the world. The 'right to enjoyment' logically includes an absolute extension of its field – up to my right to enjoy the bodies of others, and to do with them as I like. The counterpart of this globalized rationality is the systematic mechanization of perverse pleasures in Sade's orgies:

> The precisely coordinated modern sporting squad, in which no member is in doubt over his role and replacement is ready for each, has its exact counterpart in the sexual teams of Juliette, in which no moment is unused, no body orifice neglected, no function left inactive. . . . The special architectonic structure of the Kantian system, like the gymnasts' pyramids in Sade's orgies and the formalized principles of early bourgeois freemasonry . . . prefigures the organization, devoid of any substantial goals, which was to encompass the whole of life. (Horkheimer and Adorno, 2002, 69)

Roland Barthes used similar terms to point out that the orgy was meant to function as a perfectly oiled mechanism, in which everyone has a part to play and nobody can be left idle:

> The Sadian machine does not stop at the automaton . . . The whole group of the living is conceived, constructed like a machine. In its canonical state . . . it

includes a substructure constructed around the basic patient . . . and saturated when all the body's sites are occupied by different partners . . .; from this basic architecture, defined by the rule of catalysis, an open apparatus extends whose sites increase whenever a partner is added to the initial group; the machine will tolerate no one's being solitary, no one remaining outside it . . . . Once in operation, it shakes and makes a bit of noise, owing to the convulsive movements of the participants . . . . There remains but to look after it, like a good overseer who paces along, lubricating, tightening, regulating, changing, etc. ('Marthe walks along the ranks; she wipes off the balls, sees to it that . . . ' etc.). (Barthes, 1976, 152–3)

This image sends us on a new track with respect to the special style deployed in *Watt*, with its long lists of permutations attempting to exhaust any situation by means of a systematic consideration of all the possible alternatives and their endless enumerations. In this context, the eponymous hero can acquire another level of reference. Watt's name cannot be simply reduced to 'What?', as is often said, as if the name just condensed the metaphysical question par excellence, Plato's Ti Esti, or 'What is it?'; for it also calls up the Scottish James Watt, the inventor of the steam engine. James Watt (1736–1819), whose father was named James Watt, and whose son was also called James Watt (which, as Beckett would say about Jacques Moran *père* and *fils*, could not create any confusion) was the contemporary both of Immanuel Kant (1724–1804) and of the Marquis de Sade (1740–1814). Watt's very name and biography – including the mythical account of how, observing a boiling kettle, he had the idea for the first efficient steam engine, with the momentous consequences we know – call up the saga of how the Industrial Revolution swept through Europe. Watt's prototype was founded on the principle of harnessing energy via a simple interaction of pistons, rods and cylinders, so that heat could be transformed into work.

As Alfred Jarry and Marcel Duchamp understood a century and a half later, it was not such a stretch to reconfigure this machine as emblematizing a sexual mechanism. Duchamp's 'bachelors' and 'brides' are rendered in quasi-technological designs that metaphorize the production of desire. From Sade's orgies to the 'Bride Laid Bare by Her Bachelors, Even', a similar ideology of erotico-technological relationships posits the *perpetuum mobile* of desire. From the Sadean orgy organized as a montage chain in an automated plant to the eternal masturbators of the nine 'malic moulds' gazing at the vaporous bride in Duchamp's *The Large Glass*, the erotic machine materializes mechanical reproducibility. According to Adorno and Horkheimer's historical reconstruction, Watt's name alludes less to scholastic 'whatness' than to a calculating but morally apathetic Reason upon which the technological revolution that allowed the bourgeoisie to own the world was founded.

Their constant criticism of Kant's system is relevant, especially when one looks at his *Metaphysics of Morals*. Kant discusses the importance of ownership, especially when it comes to sexuality, and gives a typical definition:

> Sexual union *(commercium sexuale)* is the reciprocal use that one human being makes of the sexual organs and capacities of another *(usus membrorum et facultatum sexualium alterius)*.
>
> For the natural use that one makes of the other's sexual organs is *enjoyment*, for which one gives itself up to the other. In this act a human being makes himself into a thing, which conflicts with the right of humanity in his own person. There is only one condition under which this is possible: that while one person is acquired by the other *as if it were a thing*, the one who is acquired acquires the other in turn. (Kant, 1996, 428–9; emphasis in original)

This deadpan evocation of marriage as mutual commodification relies on Kant's formalism: the law is the law only when it is devoid of content. Any human consideration must be excluded. What matters is the simple conformity of practical reason to maxims that function like general axioms. Juliette is thus more logical than Kant when she draws consequences neglected by the philosopher: the order of society can justify crime if crime is accomplished in accordance with universal maxims. The law should regulate all actions and include all sorts of pleasures and transgressions.

Beckett's vision of a sadistic god in *Watt* thus corresponds to the view put forward by Klossowski, who, as we have seen, takes a more psychoanalytic route and highlights Sade's hatred of the Mother. According to his reading, this matricidal hatred is accompanied by a mystical cult of the orgasm, a cult underpinned by nostalgia for a lost original light. The enjoyment lost by humans is still the prerogative of an evil divinity, an utterly cruel god whom the Sadean Libertines try to emulate in their exhausting rounds of tortures and orgies. Klossowski links this negative theology with a different practice of writing. As he argues, Sade should not be seen as a 'pervert' or a 'monster', but above all as a writer. A boring and repetitive writer, to be sure, but a writer who allows us to understand the link between perverse fantasies and the absolute *jouissance* of God as the radical Other. Here is how he describes Sade's writing in *Sade My Neighbor:*

> The parallelism between the apathetic reiteration of acts and Sade's descriptive reiteration again establishes that the image of the act to be done is represented each time not only as though it had never been performed but also as though it had never been described. This reversibility of the same process inscribes the presence of *nonlanguage* in language; it inscribes a foreclosure of language by language. (Klossowski, 1991, 41)

Within the 'foreclosure' achieved by such a repetitive writing, we hesitate between the fantasy of an eternal outrage against a Mother Nature and an approximation of the excessive enjoyment of an evil God. Sade points to the dark side of humanitarian ethics by positing man's universality in relation to a caricature of the law. Sade and Beckett agree on the need to launch a transgressive language capable of questioning the definition of humanity. The serial writing deployed by *Watt* transforms an infantile rage facing the mother's body into the bland serenity of pseudo-rationality, which is called 'ataraxy':

> Watt suffered neither from the presence of Mr. Knott, nor from his absence. When he was with him, he was content to be with him, and when he was away from him, he was content to be away from him. Never with relief, never with regret, did he leave him at night, or in the morning come to him again.
>
> This ataraxy covered the entire house-room, the pleasure-garden, the vegetable garden, and of course Arthur. (Beckett, 1953, 207–208)

This ataraxy, another version of 'apathy', combines the Sadean ideal of impassiveness in the most extreme enjoyments, and the Kantian idea of a regulation of reason by itself. The main question posed by *Watt* is a Sado-Kantian question: 'But what was this pursuit of meaning in this indifference to meaning?' (Beckett, 1953, 75)

If we agree to read *Watt* as a Kantian novel doubling as a Sadean fiction, one consequence is that we have to be attentive to the metaphors connecting rational knowledge to a machine that barely hides relations of domination, fear or indifference: 'Too fearful to assume himself the onus of a decision, said Mr. Hackett, he refers it to the frigid machinery of a time-space relation' (Beckett, 1953, 21). Anticipating Lucky's parody of rational discourse in *Waiting for Godot* as a way of sending up even the Hegelian and Marxist dialectics of the master and the slave, the language of *Watt* stages a repetitive foreclosure of the law. Sade and Beckett denounce the dark side of universalistic ethics. If man is defined by an unconditional rapport to the law, then a welcome breath of fresh air allows its subversion to remind us of the reverse of the subject, its determination from behind as it were. A cruel or simply hilarious parody attacks the reverse of the subject, inverts respect by a blasphemous inversion. The law becomes a mere projection of the obscene and boundless *jouissance* of an evil Other. The risk, never avoided by Sade, is that his Libertines devote their lives to an exacting approximation of a divine *jouissance* whose slaves they become. Beckett offers a different view of excess, excess irremediably mediated by semantic serialism.

Watt never tries *being* Mr Knott, and the undemanding acquiescence of the main character is one of the mainsprings of Beckett's dark humour. However, when Beckett decided to write in French after the war, he moved away from the negative theology predicated on a perverse and evil God. Finding new resources in a different idiom, he became the writer of inner dialogism, a dialogism that would interiorize the tortures that Sade projected on his endless pool of victims. Beckett's Sadeism would shift from an uneasy negotiation between pathology and theology and turn into a perfect device to make fun of the domination of pure Reason.

3 Sade's Unreason

Let us go back to the *Temps modernes*, in which Beckett had been able to read Simone de Beauvoir's essay on Sade that foregrounds her ambivalence facing the growing cult of the 'divine Marquis'. In July 1946, Beckett published the first half of his story 'Suite', expecting the second half to appear in October, which did not happen, much to his dismay; he blamed this decision on Simone de Beauvoir, then the editor of the review. In October 1947, the *Temps modernes* published Blanchot's 'A la rencontre de Sade', which began as a review of Klossowski's recent book *Sade mon prochain*. Soon after, in 1947, Georges Bataille, whom Beckett had met a few times, published in his own review *Critique*, in which he would review *Molloy*, his two important essays on Sade, beginning with 'Le secret de Sade'. While Bataille and Blanchot were ostensibly responding to Klossowski's theses, they were actually moving in different directions. Beckett understood this when he praised Blanchot but criticized Klossowski's interpretation, an interpretation that he found too religious or theological at a time when he was trying to move beyond the impasse of *Watt*. The point that he wanted to stress was not Sade's inverted religion, but on the contrary his resolute atheism, his frank sexual materialism, and the consequent critique of 'normal' sexuality. As Blanchot saw it, Sade launched a sort of 'terror' in literature, which offered a good equivalent to Hegel's interpretation of the Terror that took place in 1793 during the French Revolution as the moment when pure and abstract Reason was unleashed and viciously turned into abstract state violence against all subjects.

Beckett was attentive to the way in which Blanchot's essay, which opens his 1949 *Lautréamont and Sade*, begins with 'Sade's Reason'. In this groundbreaking text, Blanchot confronts Sade's teeming contradictions in a magisterial manner:

> At every moment [Sade's] theoretical ideas set free the irrational forces with
> which they are bound up. These forces both excite and upset the thought by an
> impetus of a kind that causes the thought first to resist and then to yield, to try
> again for mastery, to gain an ascendancy, but only by liberating other dark

forces by which, once again the ideas are carried away, side-tracked and perverted. The result is that all that is said is clear but seems at the mercy of something that has not been said. Then, a little further on, what was concealed emerges, is recaptured by logic but, in its turn, obeys the movement of a still further hidden force. (Blanchot, 1995, 75–6)[17]

Having grasped the rationale of this perverted logic, Blanchot formalizes the paradox of Sade's doctrine in those terms:

[H]e draws up a kind of Declaration of the Rights of Eroticism, with for a fundamental principle this idea, applying equally to men and women. 'What harm do I do, what offence do I commit, if I say to a beautiful creature I meet: "Lend me the part of your body that can give me an instant's satisfaction, and enjoy, if so pleases you, the part of mine you prefer."' To Sade such a proposition is irrefutable. ... But what does he conclude from that? Not that it is wrong to do violence against anyone and use them for pleasure against their will, but that no one, so as to refuse him, can plead as excuse an exclusive attachment or 'belonging to anyone'. (76–7)

Blanchot sums up a maxim that can never become universal. Jacques Lacan formulated this maxim as follows: '"I have the right of enjoyment (*jouissance*) over your body", anyone can say to me, "and I will exercise this right without any limit to the capriciousness of the exactions I may wish to satiate with your body"' (Lacan, 2006, 648; slightly modified). We recognize Sade's black humour, a humour in which one discerns an imperceptible sliding from the rational to the merely reasonable, and then to the pathological. The subversive impact of such formulations lies in their debunking of the idea of reciprocity, a term often taken as a measure of intersubjective relationships. Sade's excessive enjoyment does not stop at mild tortures, for it often entails the dismemberment of the chosen victim, which proves that subjectivity cannot be predicated on reciprocity. Sade's perversity dispels that illusion, for the point of the formulation is to resist subjective reversal. Sade tells us that human desire is insatiable and negates reciprocity. The structure of desire as such is predicated upon a death drive that is absolute, and therefore knows no ethical bounds. What is reached by Sadean heroes and heroines is a radical freedom that combines the intensity of passion with the passivity of ataraxy. As Horkheimer and Adorno had clearly seen, Sade called this central passivity that concentrates all energy 'apathy'. After them, Blanchot also notes that the very notion develops a paradoxical logic: 'Sade has recourse to a very coherent idea to which he gives the classical name of apathy. Apathy is the spirit of negation as applied to a man who has chosen to be sovereign. It

---

[17] Blanchot's essay was initially published in *Les Temps modernes* in October 1947 as 'A la rencontre de Sade'.

is in some way the cause or principle of energy' (Blanchot, 1995, 95). The paradoxical freedom afforded by the death drive can be seen at work in many texts Beckett wrote after the war.

3.1 *Eleutheria*

The Greek word *eleutheria*, meaning freedom, the title of Beckett's first French play, keeps its foreign sound because the term suggests something like an excess, or eleutheromania. The play introduces an innovative concept of the stage, never to be used again by Beckett, by dividing it into two sides; Victor Krap, the absent object of the attentions of the others, is on stage and quite visible all the time even if he rarely intervenes. Victor has well-off parents but refuses to see them or talk to them. His main symptom is an enthusiastic passion for freedom. However, one important difference from Murphy's wish to be free is that Victor's statements are pathetically muddled and also self-cancelling: 'If I was dead, I wouldn't know I was dead. That's the only thing I have against death. I want to enjoy my death [*jouir de ma mort*]. That's where liberty lies: to see oneself dead' (Beckett, 1996, 149). However, he is obliged to speak and reveal the incoherence of his position under duress: if he remains silent, he is going to be tortured – a threat that causes panic as soon as he understands it is real.

Victor's last name enhances the atmosphere of scatological farce, soon confirmed by the name of Doctor Piouk. Victor's first name adds the suggestion of a Pyrrhic victory: his eagerly sought freedom hides a disturbing death wish. On top of that, this self-defeating victory will only trigger repeated aggressions from the other characters. While Murphy was an object of universal desire, Victor's resistance brings about loathing, contempt or just misplaced curiosity from his interlocutors. Act III forcefully introduces the theme of torture when an audience member brings in a Chinese torturer called Chouchi. His role is to make Victor speak. The Glazier, a slightly more compassionate character, voices an objection:

GLAZIER: We can't torture him (*le martyriser*).
SPECTATOR: Why not?
GLAZIER: It isn't done.
SPECTATOR: Since when?
GLAZIER: I couldn't.
SPECTATOR: Nor could I.
GLAZIER: So?
SPECTATOR: You'll see. (*He turns round to the box*) Chouchi! Come down
             here. (*Chouchi comes down on to the stage and advances*

> *with a broad oriental smile.*) You've got the picture? (*The
> smile grows broader.*) Have you got the pincers? (*Chouchi
> displays the pincers. To the Glazier*): Tell him.

GLAZIER: Victor! (*He shakes him*) You *must* talk, now.

(Beckett, 1996, 141)

Victor does not understand the danger until the threat is spelled out, for until
now he seems to have taken Chouchi for a mere hallucination:

GLAZIER: This time it's serious. They're going to pull your nails out. (*to
            Chouchi*): Aren't you?

CHOUCHI: Jlust a flew nails at flirst.

GLAZIER   (*To Victor*): You hear? Just a few nails first. *Victor raises his
            head, sees the Chinese, the smile, the pincers, recoils in
            terror.* (142)

Victor screams that he hasn't done anything wrong, and Chouchi exhibits
a catheter. This last sight convinces Victor that he is going to be tortured horribly
if he does not talk. The Glazier, too, warns Victor that unless he begins
explaining his position, he will be tortured. But he leaves the action to the
Spectator, whom he later calls 'a suburban sub-Socrates' (158). Here, the
Spectator embodies a radical demand for meaning and cannot stand the frustra-
tion that the main character is causing. By the end of the third act, we all want to
hear Victor's explanation, his conflicted rationale for his choice of a non-life.

Once Victor begins confessing, however, he again deflects the main issue; he
talks about his childhood, the impossibility of knowing another person, the way
'saints, madmen, martyrs, victims of torture' never elicit sympathy because
their torments are not perceived as such, but merely evoke 'horror and pity'
(Beckett, 1996, 145). The Spectator refuses to waste his time with the account of
this 'negative anthropology' (147), although by now we understand that the
story of Victor's non-life is the account of his life. When Victor attempts to go
further, he foregrounds his desperate quest for freedom. His refusal to live like
most people is predicated upon a radical wish to be free. In short, his life has
been 'consumed by its own liberty' (147).

Victor blurts out two more incoherent speeches, adding that he cannot
consider confessing, even under torture. When Chouchi comes near once
more, Victor shoots back: 'Can you really take account of what I say under
constraint? Are you as screwed up as that?' (Beckett, 1996, 148 ; the original is :
'Vous pouvez vraiment tenir compte de ce que je dis sous la contrainte ? Vous
êtes foutus à ce point?'; 1995b, 147). This anguished interrogation will recur
time and again in Beckett's work, and returns with poignant urgency in later
prose texts like 'As the Story Was Told' and plays such as *What Where*. They

surface most explicitly in *Rough for Radio II*, a radio play in which the desire to know the most intimate truth of a given subject ends up generating a monstrous and terrifying absurdity.

However, in *Eleutheria*, once Victor has admitted that his freedom boils down to seeing himself dead, he has negated the 'truth' that he was trying to conceal. What he has blurted out, precisely because he was under duress, is not necessarily truer than anything else. What he is forced to confess might be any odd story invented in order to be left alone. Here, Victor's nihilism dovetails with a radical scepticism about truth. It deploys once more the systematic negativism that had been displayed earlier by the cynical Doctor Piouk. In Act I, Piouk launches an impassioned tirade against generation and birth. It parodies both the rantings of Sade's Libertines, who profess their hatred of the family and reproduction, and the teachings of Schopenhauer about the constant pain generated by life. Piouk has found an original solution for the problems of the human species: the pure prohibition of reproduction.

> I would ban reproduction. I would perfect the condom and other devices and bring them unto general use. I would establish official teams of abortionists, controlled by the State. I would apply the death penalty to any woman guilty of giving birth. I would drown all newborn babies. I would militate in favour of homosexuality, and would myself set the example. And to speed things up, I would encourage euthanasia by all possible means (Beckett, 1996, 44–5).

Hearing this, Madame Krap replies eagerly: 'I was born too early' (45). Halfway between Malthus and Sade, Piouk's programme aims at stopping the propagation of that wretched species, the human race. As Borges's philosopher had it, mirrors and paternity are abominable because they reproduce the human species (1998, 69). By contrast, Victor's negative anthropology appears after all preferable to those politics of human negation and extinction.

3.2 The French Short Stories

These flashes of dark humour are not exceptional if we consider them in the context of the short stories written in French at the time. *Eleutheria* was written directly in French between January and February 1947. Beckett did not find the time to be concise enough, which is why the play tends to meander off. This was not the case with his French stories, such as 'La Fin', begun in English and completed in French in May 1946, 'L'expulsé', or 'Premier Amour' (October 1946). 'Le Calmant' followed in December 1946. A similar theme runs through these stories: a staunch refusal to allow any procreation or reproduction of the human species. It is nowhere more visible than in 'First Love', in which a circular pattern makes the narrator repeat a sudden departure from his father's house at the beginning of the narrative, which then takes the form of his headlong flight from the apartment he has shared for a while with a prostitute who was his 'first love'; this abrupt departure is triggered by the fact that she just told him that she is pregnant. He is not overjoyed: 'Look, she said, stooping over her breasts, the haloes are darkening already. I summoned up my remaining strength and said, Abort, abort, and they'll blush like new' (Beckett, 1995a, 44). Nevertheless, the narrator stays for a little longer. But when the actual birth is announced, he feels the compulsion to leave, rushing to retrieve his old clothes and running away, followed by the sound of the birth cries that echo as far as the street, and that he keeps hearing years later.

In this cynical love story, it seems that the man has been raped by the woman, as had also happened to Belacqua at the beginning of *Dream*: 'I woke next morning quite worn out, my clothes in disorder, the blanket likewise, and Anna beside me, naked naturally. One shudders to think of her exertions. . . . I looked at my member. If only it could have spoken! Enough about that. It was my night of love' (Beckett, 1995a, 42). The dead ends of love are explored in more depth in *How It Is*, although the view remains bleak.

In 'The Expelled', the narrator betrays total revulsion facing children. Once, on being forced by a policeman to walk on the pavement, he considers crushing a child to death: 'I would have crushed him gladly. I loathe children, and it would have been doing him a service, but I was afraid of reprisals. Everyone is a parent, that is what keeps you from hoping' (Beckett, 1995a, 51). Then he launches into a vicious tirade about lynching children, which fills him with sadistic glee. Beckett was to develop this idea more forcibly and subtly in *All That Fall* by strongly insinuating Mr Rooney had killed a young child in a train, in a sort of Gidean gratuitous murder. At the end, Rooney drops a ball that, we gather, belonged to the dead child – a tell-tale sign in what could almost be a detective story hidden in a radio play. The last words spoken by Jerry, a small boy himself, are ominous: 'It was a little child fell out of the carriage, Ma'am. (*Pause.*) On the line, Ma'am. (*Pause.*) Under the wheels, Ma'am' (Beckett, 1996, 199).

What stands out in these stories is that the rejection of 'normal' or reproduct-ive sexuality is accompanied by an exploration of same-sex attraction. This theme looms large in 'The Calmative' when we see the narrator kissing another man, an inquisitive and aggressive person it seems, and only on the brow (Beckett, 1995a, 74). This recurs in *Mercier and Camier*, and more clearly in the French version from 1946. The two friends share the favours of Helen, a prostitute, but several passages hint at mutual masturbation, and in one we have an uncharacteristically lyrical scene. This is the only time Beckett comes close to Sade's enthusiastic descriptions of orgies:

> They passed a peaceful night, for them, without debauch of any kind. All
> next day they spent within doors. Time tending to drag, they manstuprated
> mildly, without fatigue. Before the blazing fire, in the twofold light of lamp
> and leaden day, they squirmed gently on the carpet, their naked bodies
> mingled, fingering and fondling with the languorous tact of hands arranging
> flowers, while the rain beat on the panes. How delicious that must have been!
> (Beckett, 1974, 71)

The brothel scenes contrast with the moments when Mercier is confronted with
his children – in one disturbing scene, he rudely sends them away after they
have come to salute him meekly (31); in another, he evokes his own marriage in
the most cynical terms, after Camier asks him what he meant by 'yes'. He
replies:

> I said yes? said Mercier. I? Impossible. The last time I abused that term was at
> my wedding. To Toffana. The mother of my children. Mine own. Inalienable.
> Toffana. You never met her. She lives on. A tundish. Like fucking a quag. To
> think it was for this hectolitre of excrement I renegued my dearest dream.
> (Beckett, 1974, 84)

Mercier expects Camier to ask what his dream consisted of, but he stays silent,
which forces Mercier to elaborate: 'That of leaving the species to get on as best
as it could without me' (84). He develops this thought in sexual terms: 'Ever
since I favour the other form, said Mercier. One does what one can, but one can
nothing. Only squirm and wriggle, to end up in the evening where you were in
the morning' (84). Indeed, sodomy was preferred by Sade as a contraceptive
way of having sex, but also as a way of bypassing sexual difference. Most of his
books and stories include a scene in which a young woman is instructed in the
art of having sex through the rear end. This position combines a greater
proximity with excrement, an element of which Sade was quite fond, with
a bestialized sexual congress that can include all participants in the orgies,
whatever their gender or preferences.

In a passage of the political tract included in 'The Philosophy in the
Bedroom', Sade attempts to claim sodomy as useful for the Revolution with
the argument that 'Nature, who places such slight importance upon the essence
that flows in our loins, can scarcely be vexed by our choice when we are pleased
to vent it into this or that avenue' (Sade, 1965, 325). Sade adds that having sex
more ferarum has one advantage: one will not contribute to the propagation of
the species: 'would it not then be possible to conclude that, far, from affronting
Nature, this vice serves her intentions, and that she is less delighted by our
procreation than we foolishly believe?' (326). All these considerations find their
way obliquely but wickedly into a passage of *Molloy*, in which the eponymous

hero tries to remember whether one of his earlier lovers, called either Ruth or Edith, was a man or a woman:

> She bent over the couch, because of her rheumatism, and in I went from behind. It was the only position she could bear, because of her lumbago. It seemed all right to me, for I had seen dogs, and I was astonished when she confided that you could go about it differently. I wonder what she meant exactly. Perhaps after all she put me in her rectum. A matter of complete indifference to me, I needn't tell you. But is it true love, in the rectum? (Beckett, 1991, 56–7)

This mock-serious question recurs in later works, such as in *How It Is*, during the narrative given under torture by Pim to the narrator, in which the decreasing intensity of sexual desire is compensated by sodomitic relationships. Pim mentions his wife, whom he called Pam or Prim, and who seemed desperate because of their failing love. She then threw herself out of the window; after this, she did not die immediately, but lingered in a hospital (Beckett, 1964, 77). One detail, the method of their coition, is of particular importance: 'Pam Prim we made love every day then every third then the Saturday then just the odd time to get rid of it tried to revive it through the arse too late she fell from the window or jumped broken column' (77). The trope of the *coitus a tergo* emblematizes the non-reproductive nature of sexuality, which for Sade is a main tenet, hence his fury at pregnant mothers, who are all mercilessly tortured and killed with their offspring in his books. Sade's role should be seen as going beyond the perversion that is associated with the term 'sadism'. Sade's lesson, what he teaches us about excess, fantasy and the non-reciprocity of desire, hinges around a rejection of the idea of the family, as we have seen, and entails cruel fantasies about its negation. Often, sodomy and incest are joined, both leading to the subversion of the foundation of human kinship and reproductive laws.

Sade's animus against families underpins one of the most sadistic passages of *The Unnamable*, when the narrator describes not only the death of his entire family – they have been poisoned by the bacillus botulinus – but also explains that he stamps about the room to destroy with his crutches the last rotting remains of his dead relatives; he then walks around in his mother's entrails. As he comments, 'the mere fact of having a family should have put me on my guard' (Beckett, 1991, 322). This aside could also refer to the Marquis de Sade's complex links with his wife, mother-in-law and children. Sadean images like this provide Beckett with the means to parody once and for all the old myth of the artist's self-generation, which, according to Stephen Dedalus in *Ulysses*, explains why Shakespeare could have been not only his own father but also his grandfather; we see this in *Texts for Nothing:* 'Yes, I was my father and I was my son ... ' (Beckett, 1995a, 103).

The desire of the ultimate artist is to be his or her own creator. This desire was known to Sade, who was an all-round artist: he sang well, he painted, he danced, he was a soldier and he wrote, and was thus not a 'simple' sadist. Indeed, Sade's artistry looks meagre if we compare him with gifted contemporaries like Jean-Jacques Rousseau or Choderlos de Laclos (the only novelist not quoted by Sade in his essay on novels).[18] However, Sade's culture is that of eighteenth-century libertinism as exemplified by *Dangerous Liaisons*, and the philosophy of materialist writers like La Mettrie, but he goes further in his cult of excess which, as we have seen, is predicated on a conflicted view of Nature as not only fundamentally evil but also impossibly reproductive, the latter aspect having to be stamped out. How can we relate to fantasies created by a perverse imagination? The very excess of Sade's imagination misleads naïve readers, who take his fictions for reality. He himself insisted on this distinction and thus replied to a critic named Villeterque that he was wrong to attribute the theses of his *Crimes of Love* to the author:

> Loathsome ignoramus: have you not yet learned that every actor in any dramatic work must employ a language in keeping with his character, and that, when he does, 'tis the fictional personage who is speaking and not the author? and that, in such an instance, 'tis indeed common that the character, inspired by the role he is playing, says things completely contrary to what the author may say when he himself is speaking? (Sade, 1987, 127–8)

However, the cumulative effect of all the Libertines' discourses subverts morality and points to the dark side of humanitarian ethics. The paradoxical consequence is that Sade's heroes are the hostages of an absolute *jouissance*. Sadean libertines accumulate murders and transgression in this effort, a sign of which is the recourse to a numerology of crime predicated on the notion that one could do more. Crime has to multiply and be multiplied. We see one of these absurd calculations in *The 120 Days of Sodom*: 'He flogs a girl, giving her one hundred lashes the first day, two hundred the second, four hundred the third, etc., etc., and ceases on the ninth day' (Sade, 1987, 592). As William S. Allen has observed, this entails that the girl will have been whipped 51,100 times (2018, 117); it is unlikely that she could survive the third or fourth day! Sade did not care about verisimilitude: no sooner are his victims dispatched than they disappear from the stage, as if they only existed to be replaced by a new one. A similar disregard for verisimilitude and mathematics marks Beckett's texts, from the crazy calculations of *Watt*, as when the text attempts to calculate the sum of the years lived by the Lynch family, to the Trilogy.

---

[18] See Sade's considerations on novels in *120 Days of Sodom* (1987, 97–119).

In both Beckett and Sade there is a relief derived from counting, from numbers and from twisted mathematics. As the Superior of the convent in which Juliette is taught about luxury tells her, she should trust great numbers: 'Fuck with the maximum possible number of men; nothing so much amuses, so much heats the brain as profusion (*grand nombre*)' (Sade, 1967a, 82). The mathematization of excess offers a key for the ending of *How It Is*. Here is one typical example:

> for number 814336 as we have seen by the time he reaches number 814337 has long since forgotten all he ever knew of number 814335 as completely as though he had never been and by the time number 814335 reaches him as we have also seen has long since forgotten all he ever knew of number 814337 vast stretch of time
>
> so true it is that here one knows one's tormentor only as long as it takes to suffer him and one's victim only as long it takes to enjoy him if as long (Beckett, 1964, 121).

For Sade as for Beckett, the repetition compulsion devours the space of fiction, submits it to a principle of exhaustive listings in order to generate the sense of an infinity from which no solace can come given the endless cycle of tortures linking victim to tormentor.

4 *Comment Sade*: The Sadean Pedagogy of Love in *How It Is*

How It Is is the text that permits us to get a glimpse of Beckett's Sadean fantasy, which should be distinguished from 'sadism'. It means a grappling with Sade's texts that does not reduce them either to pathology or literature, but is capable of assessing their power of transgression. It derives from the process by which Beckett kept annotating, rewriting and commenting on Sade's texts. I am alluding here to the French title of *Comment c'est*, the 1961 novel translated as *How It Is*. While Beckett puns on 'Commencer' ('to begin') and on 'Comment c'est' ('How it is'), he engages with one of his most developed Sadean rewritings. Once more, the influence of Sade is mediated by Beckett's favourite Italian poets, Dante and Leopardi.

The term 'sadism' is mentioned in the second section of the novel, which depicts the narrator's life with Pim. Pim is an old man who crawls in the mud like all the others 'down there' in the muddy hell that is the main stage of the text, and whom the narrator tortures mercilessly. He does this with the aim of making Pim sing and tell stories to him. The passage describing the cruel lessons inflicted on Pim develops a funny passage in *Molloy* when the narrator explains the communication system he has devised to talk to his mother, with knocks going from one to four, on her skull. The difference with *How It Is* is that the mode of communication becomes rather cruel: instead of blows on the head, we have a litany of nails digging into armpits and a metal can opener savaging an old man's anus:

> first lesson theme song I dig my nails into his armpits right hand right pit he cries I withdraw them thump with fist on skull his face sinks in the mud he cries cease end of first lesson

> second lesson same theme nails in armpit cries thump on skull silence end of second lesson all that beyond my strength

> but this man is no fool he must say to himself I would if I were he what does he require of me or better still what is required of me that I am tormented thus and the answer sparsim little by little vast tracts of time

> not that I should cry that is evident since when I do I am punished instanter sadism pure and simple no since I may not cry

> something perhaps beyond my powers assuredly not this creature is no fool one senses that

> what is not beyond my powers known not to be beyond them song it is required therefore that I sing

> what if I were he I would have said it seems to me in the end to myself but I may be mistaken and God knows I'm not intelligent otherwise I'd be dead (Beckett, 1964, 62–3).

In this passage, the narrator supposes Pim to be capable of logical deduction. The French original has: 'il doit se dire je me mets à sa place que veut-il de moi en me martyrisant ainsi' (Beckett, 1961, 79). The phrase 'je me mets à sa place' highlights the ability of the narrator to think by proxy, imagining what Pim should deduce from his relentless tortures, but also to imagine himself being tortured. These tortures have an aim, which means that they are not 'pure and simple sadism'. Pim is not allowed to scream – this right being still granted to victims in Sade's fictions – because the torturing process will not be enjoyed for itself but as pedagogy. However, other versions suggest a more deliberate erotic enjoyment of the act of attacking the old man's anus with the sharp blade of a can opener: 'fire in the rectum how surmounted reflections on the passion of pain' (Beckett, 1964, 38).

In the previous passage, Pim's extra punishment if he screams when tortured should initiate a chain of thought reaching a conclusion: he is not tortured out of pure sadism, because the vicious narrator requests something from him, first a song, then some stories about his 'life above'. It is clear that the narrator will not put himself in the place of the other whom he tortures – we meet the same impossibility of a reversible ethics upon which Sade's system found its limits –

unless he himself becomes the victim of a forthcoming torturer, which seems to be the rule in this muddy hellhole.

Here, Latin words like *sparsim* and *instanter* replace the usual French terms *éparse* and *aussitôt*, with the effect of making the inner monologue approximate the bland legalese of a true pervert. In many passages that sound a similar theme, the vocabulary and the tone are reminiscent of Sade. This is the case for the 'excitations' that are to be gathered in a 'table', which brings us back to a systematic codification of all possible tortures, much as Sade codified the passions in *The 120 Days of Sodom*. These tortures create a code aiming at eliciting songs or stories:

> table of basic stimuli [*excitations de base*] one sing nails in armpit two speak blade in arse three stop thump on skull four louder pestle on kidney
>
> five softer index in anus six bravo clap athwart arse seven lousy same as three eight encore same as one or two as may be. (Beckett, 1964, 69)

What does Beckett mean when he rejects the notion of 'pure and simple sadism'? One might distinguish between vulgar sadism, the perversion that consists in enjoying a victim's pain in itself, and literary sadism, that is an effect of writing. Indeed, the first lesson teaches Pim that he must not cry out even when he feels pain. The paragraphs that follow explain why:

> all with the right hand I've said this and the left all this time vast stretch of time it holds the sack I've said this heard it said now in me that was without quaqua on all sides murmured it in the mud it holds the sack beside Pim's left hand my thumb has crept between his palm and folded fingers
>
> script and then Pim's voice till he vanishes end of part two leaving only part three and last (69).

This accounts for the huge reflexivity of the text – the narrator always quotes something that he has heard said or that has already been written; he is also writing a script by inscribing a text in uppercase letters with a can opener on the bleeding flesh of Pim. We can distinguish sadism as a regressive moment in the discovery of anal drives from the Sadism that derives from reading texts by Sade.

Most commentators of *How It Is* have stressed the Sadean tonality of the tortures, whose regular repetition ends up creating some unease. Not everyone shares Alain Badiou's equanimity when he presents *How It Is* as leading to a new opening to the Other and an abandonment of an earlier solipsism. As he aptly sums up, there are four positions offered to subjects in the novel:

(1) To wander in the dark with a sack.
(2) To encounter someone in the active position, pouncing on them in the dark. This is the so-called 'tormentor's' position.

(3) To be abandoned, immobile, in the dark, by the one encountered.

(4) To be encountered by someone in a passive position (someone pounces on you while you are immobile in the dark.) This is the position of the so-called 'victim.' It is this fourth position that the voice is not able to say, thus leading to the axiom of the three quarters concerning the relationship between truth and speech. (Badiou, 2003, 26)

Badiou refuses to see a hierarchy and insists that in theory all subjects will sooner or later come to be in the position of victims – here is something like an egalitarian reversibility, even if this does not entail total reciprocity. Is Badiou correct in assuming that Beckett is 'careful to warn us that there is something exaggerated, something falsely pathetic in these conventional denominations' of 'tormentor' and 'victim'? (26). The aim of the encounter is, as we know, a violent demand for a story of the 'life above'; that is an echo of what took place in the usual world, before the transformation of the subjects into crawling creatures in the dark and the mud. Badiou imagines that it is a woman who first travels in the dark, and that 'whoever is immobile in the dark is a man' (27).

This leads Badiou to stress the function of love in the novel, a term that he takes at face value. In his reading, Beckett's couples should not be read as asexual or homosexual, but as foregrounding the 'generic', that is, the most universal features in human beings: as the text says, 'humanity regained' (Beckett, 1964, 27). However, Badiou contradicts himself when he adds that whoever pounces on a victim is 'masculine', whoever is a victim is 'feminine' (Badiou, 2003, 65). However we are told that Pim is a man, who is endowed with testicles. As soon as the narrator has assured himself of the presence of testicles in Pim's body, he confesses that he too is an old man:

> good a fellow-creature more or less but man woman girl or boy cries have neither certain cries sex nor age I try to turn him over on his back no right side still less the left less still my strength is ebbing good good I'll never know Pim but on his belly
>
> all that I say it as I hear it every word always and that having rummaged in the mud between his legs I bring up finally what seems to me a testicle or two the anatomy I had
>
> as I hear it and murmur in the mud that I hoist myself if I may say so a little forward to feel the skull it's bald no delete the face it's preferable mass of hairs all white to the feel that clinches it he's a little old man we're two little old men something wrong there (Beckett, 1964, 54).

Badiou is right to state that *How It Is* revolves around the story of the 'life in common' uniting Pim and the narrator, but one should not forget that both are old and male. Unlike *Murphy*, in which the hero leaves Celia in spite of their reciprocal feelings of love to find company among the inmates of the psychiatric asylum, a quest shown to be abortive and doomed from the start, *How It Is* makes room for love among two people. However, this entails a certain feminization of Pim, an old man who will be called 'cunt' quite systematically. This feminization is mediated by recurrent motives that obsess the narrator, the can opener and the buttocks. The narrator, afraid of losing his precious can opener in the mud, finds a convenient hiding place:

> between the cheeks of his arse not very elastic but still sufficiently there it's in safety saying to myself I say as I hear it that with someone to keep me company I would have been a different man more universal
>
> not there lower down between the thighs it's preferable the point downward and only the little bulb protruding of the uniform handle there it's out of danger saying to myself too late a companion too late
>
> second lesson then second series same principle same procedure third fourth so on vast stretch of time till the day that word again when stabbed in the arse instead of crying he sings his song what a cunt this Pim damn it all confuse arse and armpit horn and steel the thump he gets then I give you my word happily he is no fool he must have said to himself what is required of me now what is the meaning of this new torment (Beckett, 1964, 67).

The narrator makes explicit the link between the castrating tool and the inner thigh, as he had announced at the beginning of Part 2, when he called Pim's voice 'this semi-castrate mutter' (51), or more clearly in French, 'murmure de demi-castrat' (1961, 64). Once Pim has been qualified as a 'cunt', which translates the more common French colloquialism of 'con' (meaning simply 'stupid'), he is associated with femininity. The repeated request for love is systematically rendered as 'Do you love me, cunt?' (1964, 90), carved in Roman capitals on his back. These words once inscribed also mark the ending of Part 2 and of the love story:

> thump on skull no point in post mortem and then what then what we'll try and see last words cut thrust a few words DO YOU LOVE ME CUNT no disappearance of Pim end of part two leaving only part three and last one can't go on one goes on as before can one ever stop put a stop that's more like it one can't go on one can't stop put a stop (90).

Love might be interpreted as a retrospective view of Pim once he has turned into a corpse, which is suggested by passages like this one: 'with me someone there with me still and me there still strange wish when the silence there still enough for me to wonder if only a few seconds if he is breathing still or in my arms already a true corpse untorturable henceforward' (Beckett, 1964, 92). Pim would then have become 'un vrai cadavre insuppliciable désormais' (1961, 113). The narrator of *How It Is* encounters the problem Sade's narratives face:

when Libertines multiply exactions against their victims, they either need characters endowed with supernatural powers of resistance to their butchery, or have to replace them in rapid sequences of quasi-identical bodies. But the goal remains that of a Saint-Fond eager to torture his victims after their physical demise, so as to generate an eternity of sufferings:

> if he wants me to leave him yes in peace yes without me there is peace yes was peace yes every day no if he thinks I'll leave him no I'll stay where I am glued to him yes tormenting him eternally yes (Beckett, 1964, 98).

One cannot think of a more effective parody of Molly's monologue in Joyce's *Ulysses* with its triumphant 'yeses' to love. One can say that *How It Is* is much darker than what Badiou surmises; the novel relentlessly narrates how the narrator finds Pim in the mud, and tortures him by his repeated lessons and then by carving words on his buttocks with a can opener.

It is only when we reach Part 3 that a rationale is given for the sadistic couplings previously described: they follow 'our justice', a phrase that is repeated several times. In a revealing paragraph, a most violent language testifies to a sort of metaphysical despair:

> the fuck who suffers who makes us to suffer who cries who to be left in peace in the dark the mud gibbers ten seconds fifteen seconds of sun clouds earth sea patches of blue clear nights and of a creature if not still standing still capable of standing always the same the same imagination spent looking for a hole that he may be seen no more in the middle of this faery who drinks that drop of piss of being and who with his last gasp pisses it to drink the moment it's someone each in his turn as our justice wills and never any end it wills that too dead or none (Beckett, 1964, 132).

Jonathan Boulter (2012) has read this passage as exemplifying Jacques Derrida's idea that justice cannot be deconstructed.[19] Much as I admire Derrida's take on 'Force of Law' and the subtlety of Boulter's posthuman reading, it seems that Derrida's definition of justice as a transcendental concept underpinning an experience of the impossible is not so relevant in this context. Against this reading, I would suggest that Beckett uses Sade's logics to question a theological world view in which 'divine' and 'justice' rhyme together, and for that reason will be rejected. Beckett's concept of justice has been reduced to a series of calculations; it adds up numbers frantically and almost randomly, which should ensure a type of universality and identical repetition of the same. The paradox embodied by this passage is that, once more, one cannot distinguish justice from Injustice. Here it seems that justice means more the law of eternal return, in the parody of

---

[19] See also Bersani and Dutoit (1993) and Cunningham (2008).

a Nietzschean idea made cruder and more sinister by generating a vision of life as a perpetual crawling through mud, muck and shit, an aimless and desperate progression from which even death cannot free us.

Beckett reveals how deeply he was fascinated by Dante's excremental passages in his *Inferno*, but also felt the need to go beyond, to radicalize the fantasy and dismantle it (see Caselli, 2005). Hence there is no clear difference between this 'piss of being' ('cette goutte de pisse d'être'; Beckett, 1961, 159) and the statement that 'we have our being in justice' ('on est dans la justice'; 150). The context is clear: 'nothing to be done in any case we have our being in justice I have never heard anything to the contrary' (Beckett, 1964, 124). The echo of the opening sentence of *Waiting for Godot* signals that 'justice' does not gesture towards an opening to the incalculable but signals a sad necessity, a mortal and moral fate. The ethical experience proposed by Beckett with a rare rigor – here, the voice uttering something 'to the contrary', the ethical voice, is silent – takes place outside the domain of justice.

Beckett's notion of justice is indebted to Dante's *contrapasso*, the idea of a homology between sins committed on earth and punishments meted out in Hell. Finding correspondences between the crimes and their punishments is a challenge that allows Dante to show his invention. If he finds powerful images exemplifying the workings of divine justice, his justice is also a matter of precise, almost mechanical, calculations. In Canto 5, we meet Minos, a 'connoisseur of sin' who coils his tail so that the number of its coils indicates the level of damnation, which in its turn determines the types of torture sinners will undergo. They are all assigned adequate torments in a perfect machinery of suffering. God's justice is impersonal and without pity: it is meted out according to a codified, if opaque, system of allegorical equivalence.

Indeed, Sade aimed at emulating this mathematization of eternal pain, while being sceptical as to the roots of a moral rationale for such a condemnation. We see this in a letter to Mademoiselle de Rousse that sketches a predicament similar to the main theme of *How It Is*: 'Wretched creatures, thrown for an instant onto this little heap of mud, must it be then that one half of the herd should persecute the other half?'[20] In darker moments, Sade pokes fun at the idea of justice, as in this passage of *The 120 Days of Sodom* which sketches a typical evolution in the orgies, the moment when Libertines decide to punish a helper; here it is the young Fanchon, who had been a trusted accomplice up to then:

> Fanchon is led into the arena, made to shit, given a hundred lashes by each of the friends, and then the Duc deftly shaves off her left nipple. She raises

---

[20] Sade, 'Lettre à Mademoiselle de Rousset', *Etudes Philosophiques,* 26 January 1782, quoted in Annie Le Brun (2014, 17).

a storm, criticizing their behavior toward her and describing it as unjust. 'Were it just', says the Duc, wiping his razor, 'it would surely fail to give us an erection.' (Sade, 1987, 642)

The cynicism of the Duke introduces a central theme in Sade, the *jouissance* of performing evil deeds that exceed any pre-arranged system of measure ordering punishments in conformity with transgressions. Sade's cult of *jouissance* requires the new jolt of an unfair and unprovoked torment. Beckett seems to believe that without excessive enjoyment, the Libertine would fall into the depressive state of Dante's *Tristi*, Sadean *ataraxia* conquered by accumulating crimes and tortures transformed into the *acedia* of the Sullen.

Acedia is evoked in Canto 7 of *Inferno*, where we meet the Sullen ones, those *Tristi*, the sad ones who have been eaten up by a sort of *tedium vitae*.[21] They have failed to pay homage to the brightness of the sun because of their inner darkness; these damned souls have been plunged into a slimy bog of wet mud, where they keep humming a hymn about their sad fate, but can hardly sing because the mud clogs their throats:

> This hymn they have to gurgle in their gullets,
> because they cannot speak it in full words.
> (Dante Alighieri, 1981, 65)

Dante's words evoke the gurgling sounds issuing from throats attempting to sing under muddy water: 'Quest' inno si gorgoglian ner la strozza' (64; see also Dante Alighieri, 1967, 474). This pervasive mud as a universal medium is a recurrent trope in *How It Is*. Mud as a substance is as nourishing (it provides liquid for the mouths of the questers) as it is suffocating, a gagging if not entirely disgusting substance. In Beckett's text, this slime is partly made up of vomit or anal refuse issuing from the narrator's anus ('quick a supposition if this so-called mud were nothing more than all our shit yes all'; Beckett, 1964, 52). Such 'quaqua' is the remainder of Lucky's diseased discourse that hesitated between logorrhoea and diarrhoea in *Waiting for Godot*. Going further, *How It Is* deploys Beckett's anal fascination with this omnipresent scatological mud that invades everything. It is truly the substance of the world 'below', which actualizes the programme contained in Leopardi's line 'e fango è il mondo', which figured as the epigraph of Beckett's *Proust*.[22]

Following this radical equation of world with mud, the characters of *How It Is* are bogged down in Napoleon's fifth element, as he described mud after the Russian campaign debacle. Here, mud and slime coalesce substantially in an

---

[21] For a good analysis of this, see Caselli (2005, 148–82).

[22] In 'A Se Stesso', Giacomo Leopardi wrote: 'Amaro e noia / La vita, altro mai nulla; e fango è il mondo' ('Life is merely bitterness and boredom, and the world is filth') (Leopardi, 2011, 234–5).

excremental vision that includes verbal matter: it connects Lucky's 'quaqua-quaqua' with derisive verbiage in German, 'Quatsch quatsch quatsch' (*Dream*; Beckett, 1992, 36). If the world is mud and language slime, one will barely distinguish them. *How It Is* presents this desperate crawling in the mud as the horizon of ontology and of ethics.

How It Is is told by a narrator who crawls through a mass of scatological mud in the dark and tortures Pim. We saw the obsessively invasive mud in Dante's *Inferno*, but in case we missed the reference, a passage distorts a famous line: 'dream come of a sky an earth an under-earth where I am inconceivable aah no sound in the rectum a redhot spike that day we prayed no further' (Beckett, 1964, 37). The reference is to Paolo and Francesca falling in love as they read a book together: 'that day we read no further' (*Inferno*, Canto 5:109). Dante and Sade have been joined for all eternity.

Distorting 'read' into 'pray', Beckett attacks religion as such, which reminds us of Beckett's hostile review of Giovanni Papini's book on Dante, *Dante Vivo*, in 1934. Papini had argued that Dante had paid for his success as a writer by failing completely in his life. He concluded that we should not reduce Dante to literature but see him as a man, which would be needed in order to love him. Beckett rebukes this sentimental view: 'But who wants to love Dante? We want to READ Dante – for example, his imperishable reference (Paolo-Francesca episode) to the incompatibility of the two operations' (Beckett, 1983, 81).

Beckett's law is the law of the text, a law of reading that replaces the Christian law of love, and which also corresponds to a Sadean universe in which love is but a brief madness. The only truth will come from writing one's most extreme fantasies without any consideration for others. Dante and Proust share a similar sadism, a point made first by Georges Bataille, who had insisted on Proust's sadism in *Literature and Evil*. Bataille always put forward Sade's base materialism, showing it hinged around the economy of excrement. He liked quoting this passage from the *Nouvelle Justine*, in which Verneuil is presented as coprophagic: 'Verneuil makes someone shit, he eats the turd, and then he demands that someone eat his. The one who eats his shit vomits; he devours her puke' (qtd. in Bataille, 1985, 95). We have seen that Beckett had referred to 'all those turds' in a letter to Duthuit (2011, 311), and he may have felt that Sade would beat him on the topic of shit, which recurs ad infinitum in *The 120 Days of Sodom*. For Bataille, this rapid exchange of rejected and abject substances defines a Freudian economy of appropriation and excretion, a necessary evil if one wants to accomplish a revolution:

> Without a profound complicity with natural forces such as violent death, gushing blood, sudden catastrophes and horrible cries of pain that

accompany them, terrifying ruptures of what had seemed immutable, the fall into stinking filth of what had been elevated – without a sadistic understanding of an incontestably thundering and torrential nature, there could be no revolutionaries, there could only be a revolting utopian senti-mentality[.] (Bataille, 1985, 101)

This will lead us to consider the more revolutionary aspects of Sade, as understood quite clearly by Beckett.

5 Sade's Dark Revolution

We saw earlier that Beckett had reservations about Peter Weiss's Marxist and Brechtian play that pits two of the most notorious actors of the French Revolution against each other: Marat, who is assassinated by Charlotte Corday at the climax of the play; Sade, who takes the scene of Marat's death, famously memorialized by David's painting, as a pretext for a play staged in the Charenton asylum. We have seen that Sade was allowed to direct plays in the asylum, in which many inmates participated. Weiss presents a more and more worried director of the clinic, Abbé de Coulmier, who at the end has to pull down the curtain given the frenzy released by the revolutionary text and the performances of sadly unhinged unprofessional actors. The play is set in 1808, a time when Napoleon, who had been made Emperor four years earlier, wanted to suppress vice and perversity and launch a new moral order. As Weiss explains (1981, 106), there was no historical basis for a meeting between Marat and Sade, though Sade had been given the task of writing and reading a memorial address for Marat's state funeral in 1793.

Sade read his 'Discours prononcé à la fête décernée par la Section des Piques aux mânes de Marat et de Le Peletier' (Speech given at the ceremony for the commemoration of Marat and Le Peletier organized by the Section des Piques) on 29 September 1793, while the guillotine was busy decapitating scores of noble suspects nearby. Then, on 25 November of the same year, Marat's body was transferred to the Panthéon in great pomp. Sade was the delegate of the Section des Piques, fully aware that the group of the Montagnards had added his name to the list of those to be sent to the guillotine. Although Weiss has taken some liberties with the true story by placing different characters in the same asylum, his historical knowledge is nonetheless accurate – the play notes, for instance, that Corday was not a Royalist but a Republican close to the Girondins, who were being eliminated by the Montagnards, of whom Marat was the most bloodthirsty.

We have seen that Beckett felt that Weiss's play was not satisfactory, but he singled out for praise the scene in which Sade arranges to be whipped in public.

This scene allows us to catch Sade in the role of willing victim; indeed, he was known to either flagellate himself or to be flagellated by servants during his orgies. Moreover, this scene accounts for a detail that has surprised most commentators: Sade's revulsion in face of the guillotine and scenes of actual murder. The young inmate who plays the role of Charlotte Corday is given a many-stranded whip with which she whips Sade's back while he faces the audience, having stripped off his shirt. He declares:

> At first I saw in the revolution a chance for a tremendous outburst of revenge // an orgy greater than my dreams
>
> (CORDAY slowly raises the whip and lashes him. SADE cowers.)
>
> But then I saw // When I sat in the courtroom myself
>
> (Whiplash. SADE gasps.)
>
> not as I had been before the accused // but as a judge // I couldn't bring myself // To deliver the prisoners to the hangman
>
> (Whiplash.)
>
> I did all I could to release them or let them escape // I saw I wasn't capable of murder
>
> (Whiplash. SADE groans asthmatically.)
>
> although murder // was the final proof of my existence //and now
>
> (Whiplash. He gasps and groans.)
>
> the very thought of it // horrifies me ...
>
> (Weiss, 1981, 48)

When Sade evokes the slaughters like those performed at the Carmelite Convent, the tumbrels full of nobles and priests taken to be executed, he concludes that they lost any meaning for him: 'all the meaning drained out of this revenge // It has become mechanical' (49). Sade condemns the revolutionary terror for which Marat was held responsible, and sounds nostalgic, regretting the moment when death was individualized; then pain was enjoyable, and not abused by a juridical system buttressed on a machine that was supposedly capable of severing the head from the body painlessly. This poignant scene of moral recantation ends with a premonition of his famous will, the request for a tomb hidden from sight: 'And when I vanish // I want all trace of my existence // To be wiped out' (50).

We know more about how Sade was allowed to stage his plays in the Charenton asylum thanks to Laure Murat's *The Man Who Thought He Was Napoléon* (2014). Murat read the archives of the Charenton clinic to throw light on the curious complicity linking the director, Coulmier, and Sade. Both were denounced as perverts and debauched by the very Catholic Royer-Collard, who then managed to take over Charenton. When he first visited the establishment, Royer-Collard was shocked by the promiscuity of the asylum, and by the fact that Sade controlled the entertainments. Sade was holding court, lending books, flattering the director in his plays and conversing with whoever wanted to come near.

Murat points out that Coulmier, the director, was in the habit of keeping a feminine harem, for life in that asylum was highly sexualized. The real Coulmier, who had nothing to do with his Hollywood metamorphosis into a good-looking priest played by Joaquin Phoenix in the film *Quills* (Coulmier was short, almost a hunchback, with severely deformed limbs, and he was sixty-seven at the time of the play), resisted as long as he could all the entreaties he received to restrain or lock up Sade.[23] One of Sade's plays led to heightened unrest and unleashed passions among the inmates, which led to their author's downfall. However, Sade had just died when the new director took over Charenton; he was spared the indignity of being sent to a more severe gaol.

What interested Brook and Weiss was the mixture of revolutionary fervour manifested by Marat and Roux, and the presence of Sade and Coulmier. The latter came from the Old Regime but endorsed republican ideals, and both were at odds with the restoration of ancient ideals of propriety by Napoleon. Moreover, one can say that their unlikely collaboration launched the practice of drama therapy to cure those who were considered insane. There were a few professional actors in Sade's plays, but most of the rest were chosen from among the inmates. The audience would be a mixture of inmates and of guests who had travelled from Paris. Sade would not only write the plays, but also act and even sing in them.

For Beckett, the problem with Brook's adaptation of Weiss's play was the uneasy coexistence of a participation theatre in the spirit of Artaud, who was one of Brook's references, and of a Brechtian 'distancing effect' that interrupts the attention of the crowd in order to analyse what is happening on the stage. We know that Beckett attended a workshop for the production of the *Theatre of Cruelty* at the London Academy of Music and Dramatic Art theatre club on 29 January 1964. Brook and Charles Marowitz had organized a workshop juxtaposing Artaud's famous programme with contemporary events.[24] In his

---

[23] This 2000 film directed by Philip Kaufman was based on a play with the same title by Doug Wright, who wrote the film script. Wright's 1995 work was awarded the Kesselring prize for best new American play. In the film, Geoffrey Rush is Sade, and Kate Winslet the young Madeleine Le Clerc.

[24] See Beckett (2014, 593 n5) for references to two articles of the *Times* on the topic of the Theatre of Cruelty and this workshop.

first manifesto for a 'Theatre of Cruelty' Artaud had included the idea of adapting a story by the Marquis de Sade, adding: 'eroticism will be transposed, figured allegorically, and disguised, going toward the violent exteriorization of cruelty, and a dissimulation of the rest' (Artaud, 2004, 565). As Knowlson tells us, one memorable night, Beckett, Edward Albee, Harold Pinter and Patrick Magee spent hours in a pub getting very drunk, 'enthusiastically discussing the Marquis de Sade' (1996, 458).

Why was Beckett disappointed with the staging of the play, when we know that the 1964 production of *Marat/Sade* garnered its load of prizes in London? It was considered a reference point for the new theatre. When Ariane Mnouchkine produced her amazing *1789* in 1974, theatre cognoscenti compared it with the innovations of Brook's staging. Brook and Mnouchkine managed the feat of creating a collective voice: for Brook, the slowly growing anger of the inmates facing the pageant of recent revolutionary history; for Mnouchkine, the collective 'legend' of what the French Revolution actually meant for the people. This was not the way Beckett's theatre was developing at the time, although he would work on similar themes in the prose text *Le Dépeupleur*.

Beckett may have smiled at the neo-Marxist optimism of Weiss, who has to introduce Jacques Roux, the radical Socialist who aspires to a just society and condemns the excesses of Marat and Sade. He is always in a straitjacket in Weiss's play, and is given the most political speeches in the first act. In the play, we see him demand granaries for the people, and the transformation of churches into schools. In fact, he was a militant for the abolition of private property and the end of any class distinction. This gained him the name of 'the enraged'. He was also for ending the war leading to the conquest of most of Europe (Weiss, 1981, 44–5), for he was indeed a pacifist – which would not have pleased Napoleon in 1808. However Roux could not have been in the Charenton asylum then; he had taken his own life in 1794, knowing that he would be guillotined for his subversive views, and also because Marat had turned against him at the last moment.

Weiss explains in his author's note that Roux, 'one of the most fascinating personalities of the revolution', has the role of 'a champion and perfectionist, an *alter ego* against whom Marat's ideas can be measured' (Weiss, 1981, 108). Indeed, at the end, Roux asks the audience to 'learn to see' and 'learn to take sides' (100). Beckett rejected such a direct appeal to the political sensibility of the audience, and had never really tried to put actual crowds on the stage. Weiss forces us to meditate on the collective movements that lead people onto the stage; he links personal events (such as those that have caused the dire symptoms the inmates suffer from) with a collective transformation of history known as the 'Revolution'. Can Sade remain in place as a hidden and cynical director? Should he be replaced by Marat, or even by Roux? This is one of the questions

Weiss poses. Beckett eschewed such crucial questions, not because he was opposed to any political theatre, but because he had a different political reading of Sade. And he found that reading in a book by Geoffrey Gorer.

Gorer, an exact contemporary of Beckett, died in 1985; this English writer had tried his hand at writing plays and novels in the 1930s but, failing to get published, became a well-known anthropologist. His first book was *The Revolutionary Ideas of the Marquis de Sade* (1934). Later in his career, he wrote accounts of trips to Africa, to Bali and to the Himalayas. He became known as an anthropologist of death, with an interest in pornography and psychoanalysis. One important essay, 'The Pornography of Death' (1955), echoes his previous work on Sade. It concludes on a prescient analysis:

> If we dislike the modern pornography of death, then we must give back to death – natural death – its parade and publicity, re-admit grief and mourning. If we make death unmentionable in polite society – 'not before the children' – we almost ensure the continuation of the 'horror comic.' No censorship has ever been really effective. (Gorer, 1955, 52)

Gorer argues that because death has become invisible, tucked away in rituals that disguise it in modern society, our repressed fascination with death emerges all the more strongly in graphic or violent representations in films, novels and the media.

We cannot know for sure when Beckett read Gorer's 1934 book on Sade. He felt that it would be useful for Patrick Magee when he was rehearsing *Marat/ Sade*. One could surmise that he read it in 1938, at the time when he was considering translating *The 120 Days of Sodom*, but it might have been only in 1964, when he asked Mary Hutchinson to lend books on Sade to Magee. At least the choice of these books cannot be due to chance. Beckett was picky, praising Maurice Heine to Duthuit while objecting to Klossowski's religious reading. Whether in 1938 or 1964, he had outgrown his juvenile fascination with decadence as monumentalized by Praz. Gorer's book offers a missing link between the first readings of Sade as 'decadent' or 'satanist', and a more political reading.

Gorer published his book one year after Praz's had appeared in English. Gorer remarks snidely that Praz may not have read *Justine* or *Juliette* carefully, or at all, for, as he notes, the extensive quotes from Sade strung together in the section of *La carne, la morte e il diavolo* overlap with the quotes from Sade already available in a book by Lafourcade on Swinburne (Gorer, 1934, 101).[25] Indeed, in the second volume of *La Jeunesse de Swinburne*, Lafourcade showed

---

[25] Gorer sends the reader to Georges Lafourcade's dissertation, *La Jeunesse de Swinburne (1837– 1867)* (1928). Lafourcade's dissertation, however, quotes an essay on Swinburne that Praz had already published in 1922. One can assume that the identical quotes are due to the fact that both critics have read *Justine* and *Juliette* with similar protocols of interpretation. No need to suspect Praz of having been lazy!

how entire passages from *Atalanta*, *Anactoria* and *Dolores* were transcriptions of Sade's texts. To be sure, Praz quotes some passages from Sade that are in Lafourcade, but other quotes from Sade in *La carne* do not originate from Lafourcade.

Other differences are more telling: unlike that of Praz, who uses literary analysis in order to reconstruct a tradition marked by 'decadence', Gorer's reading of Sade is historical and political; where Praz insists on Sade's perverse turn, Gorer stresses Sade's unleashing of revolutionary energy, and his critique of the rapacity of the powerful tyrants who oppress the people. Gorer praises Sade not only for having been one of the forces of dissolution of the *ancien régime* ushering in the French Revolution, but also for having been quickly disillusioned with its excess, all the while refusing to collaborate with Napoleon once he had seized power. Gorer believed that Sade deployed 'Revolutionary Ideas' and proves it from many close readings of his texts, not just from his biography.

However, Sade's biography is used in two crucial moments of Gorer's narrative. First, there is the famous day when Sade started screaming that prisoners were being executed in the Bastille, which led to his being sent to Charenton. On 2 July 1789, Sade shouted out from his cell to the crowd outside that innocent prisoners were being slaughtered, creating a disturbance which led to his transfer to the insane asylum at Charenton on 4 July. The governor of the Bastille stated that if 'Monsieur de Sade was not removed tonight from the Bastille, I cannot be answerable to the King for the safety of the building' (qtd. in Gorer, 1934, 53). Indeed, the governor was to lose his life during the storming of the Bastille, and his head was carried on a pike during the events that took place ten days later on 14 July. This was the first bloody event leading to the French Revolution, and one can assert without too much exaggeration that Sade was instrumental in making it happen. The second moment is when Sade, who was the speaker for the section des Piques, of which Marat was also a member, refused to take revenge on the Président and Madame de Montreuil, his father-in-law and mother-in-law who had persecuted him for three decades. In a magnanimous gesture, he refused to sign the latter's death warrant. This was interpreted as weakness, and soon he found himself in gaol with the moderates (Gorer, 1934, 57–8).

The Sade who emerges from Gorer's account is more interesting and subtle than what we find in most English-language analyses, and much more documented than the wholesale endorsement given by the Surrealists. Gorer, who had read Freud, refuses to give the epithet of 'sadist' to Sade, and prefers to consider him as a writer carried away by a wish to present a scientific study of sexual passions, which include all perversions, and by a deep misanthropy. Here is how he presents this:

> Lear and Timon are but pale shadows compared to de Sade at this epoch. His aim is no less than strip every covering, both mental and physical, off man and expose him to our disgusted gaze as the mean and loathsome creature he is. It is the supreme blasphemy. Our gods you may attack, individuals you may show to be monsters, but to attack the human race is unforgivable. Even the paler 'scientific' exposures of the Viennese psychoanalysts have called forth the most indignant remonstrances; no wonder de Sade, with his cold and objective exhibition of the most carefully hidden corner of our unconscious minds, of our daily weaknesses and meannesses, has been tracked and pursued by authority all over the world. (Gorer, 1934, 88)

Beckett might have subscribed to such a programme. However, Gorer is more political than psychoanalytic in his readings. He understands a feature that most readers have missed: the characters presented as diehard libertines in the novels are satires of the powerful, whose unleashed perversions often aim at a reactionary regime denounced by Sade's narratives. Gorer is one of the first exegetes (beside Maurice Heine) who saw that the 'ghastly projects' that Sade puts in the mouths of his 'reactionary "fascist" characters' should not be taken to represent his own desires, but on the contrary to show *ab absurdo* the mistake they make about freedom and sexuality. In 1934, Gorer multiplies parallels with the political issues of the day, for he sees in Sade's works an anti-fascist machine. This was a point that had been made just a few years earlier by Bataille, and was disseminated in texts that only circulated in a small circle of dissident Surrealists (see Bataille, 1985). Like Bataille, Gorer sees in Sade's novels a double message: a call for insurrection in the name of amoral excess, along with parodies of the delirious megalomania of proto-fascist speakers.

Gorer quotes the Preface to *Justine*, in which Sade argues that writers have the right to say anything. Sade's freedom entailed a critique of sexuality and did not spare religion. Like Beckett and Heine, Gorer appreciates the 'elegant' *Dialogue between a Priest and a Dying Man* as offering a 'well-reasoned piece of dialectic' that he finds 'moderate and dignified in its language' (1934, 119). He singles out a few witticisms – here is one from *Juliette*:

> It is amusing that the Jacobins in the French Revolution wanted to destroy the altars of a God who used absolutely their language, and even more extraordinary that those who detest and wish to destroy the Jacobins do so in the name of a God who speaks like the Jacobins. If this is not the nec plus ultra of human absurdity I should like to know what it is. (qtd. in Gorer, 1934, 121)

Gorer compares Juliette with Lenin, who objected to religion as being the opium of the people. For him, Sade attacks all religions because he sees that they harboured the basis for distorted ideologies. *Juliette*, in which we discover a series of corrupt leaders and legislators, seems most relevant in this regard, for it 'exposes a system of corruption and intrigue which often reads like a description of the United States today, together with a hard-heartedness and sanctimonious cynicism which might have served as a model to Hitler's Germany or our own National Government' (Gorer, 1934, 132–3). Gorer adds this prescient remark: 'The astounding feature of the book is its modernity; it is difficult to realize that it is the eighteenth century and not the twentieth century he is describing' (133). Saint-Fond explains that he plans to multiply criminal exactions above all because he is afraid of a revolution, which presages Hitler and Mussolini. Gorer never doubts that Sade was an authentic revolutionary, a republican disgusted with the system of the ancient regime, and moreover shocked by the mechanized murder of the Terror in 1793.

Had Beckett remembered this positive appreciation when he saw the shortcomings of Peter Weiss's disqualification of Sade as a revolutionary figure? He saw how limited it was to present Sade as a cynical manipulator of his fellow inmates' repressed sexual urges. The least one can say is that throughout his writings, Sade kept attacking the links between tyranny, religion and the repression of sexuality. Sade brought to the new world his dark enlightenment, but also insisted on the equality between men and women, which is why his two best novels, *Justine* and *Juliette*, highlight their feminine heroines (a point made by Angela Carter in *The Sadeian Woman*, 1978). Gorer notes that *Juliette* is a first-person narrative that enlists the reader's sympathies for the wicked heroine who thrives in her depravation, whereas the *Nouvelle Justine* has to be in the third person, since she dies at the end, struck by a thunderbolt, but also because distance is needed to take in her misfortunes.

Gorer had read Sade closely and did not neglect humorous stories like 'The Mystified Magistrate'. At some point, a magistrate who has been made to drink too much cannot remember what term best characterizes the consequences of justice. Stuttering, he blurts out a hidden obscenity, '*merde*' emerging as the key to justice: 'il faut être sévère, la sévérité est la fille de la justice . . . et la justice est la mère de . . . je vous demande pardon, Madame, il y a des moments où la mémoire me fait faux bond' (qtd. in Gorer, 1934, 79; 'One has to be severe, severity is the daughter of Justice, and Justice is the mother of . . . I beg your pardon, Madam, at times my memory fails me'). Sade's pun may have generated another untranslatable pun found among the Addenda to *Watt*: '*Die Merde hat mich wieder*' (Beckett, 1953, 250). Splicing Goethe's lofty 'Die Erde hat mich wieder' ('The earth has me again') from *Faust* with Sade's base materialism and bathetic atheism, both underpinning a recurrent anal obsession, Beckett gives us a neat reminder that Mother Earth includes manure as well.

6 Eternally Reversible Catastrophes

Beckett used a similar technique to that of *Marat/Sade,* with its device of a play within a play, when he composed *Catastrophe* in order to launch a clear political critique. He combined this technique with an insight provided by Roland Barthes, who notes the way Sade's bodies have to be fully lit, in an excessive but neutral atmosphere that risks making them all identical:

> Just as the bodies of Sadian subjects are insipid, since they are totally beautiful (beauty is only a *class*), so the buttocks, the breath, the sperm find an immediate individuality of language. Captured in its insipidness, its abstraction ... the Sadian body is in fact a body seen from a distance in the full light of the stage; it is merely a *very well lit* body the very illumination of which, even, distant, effaces individuality (skin blemishes, ill-favored complexion), but allows the pure charm to come through .... It is this abstract body's theatricality which is rendered in dull expressions (*perfect body, ravishing body, fit for a painting,* etc.), as though the description of the body had been exhausted by its (implicit) staging: perhaps it is the function of this touch of hysteria which underlies all theater (all lighting) to combat this touch of fetishism contained in the very 'cutting' of the written sentence. (Barthes, 1976, 127–8)

In a similar dialectical tension between words and images, Beckett's play begins by presenting an obnoxious and tyrannical director who terrorizes his secretary as he wants to achieve precise effects in the staging of a living statue, using the unwilling participation of an old man who looks more like a political prisoner than a hired extra. Huffing and puffing, claiming to be in a hurry, the director lingers on details of colour and gesture while checking his watch, eager to go to a political meeting after the theatrical business has been settled to his satisfaction. His young assistant, who reminds us of the assistant in *Rough for Radio II*, arranges the poses for the old man standing on a podium. The result will be an opaque allegory, an old man with his hands joined as in prayer.

One perceives links between *Rough for Radio II* and *Catastrophe.* In the radio piece and the play, a similar structure is repeated: the animator or the director plays the role of the tyrannical agent, with a young secretary as helper, witness and accomplice. The victim is an older man, who will either reveal a secret when blurting out something banal or poetic, or take on a pose. There is an audible weapon in *Rough for Radio II,* a 'bull's pizzle' (Beckett, 1986, 275) that we hear resounding; this was one of the favoured instruments of discipline for the helpers of the Libertines in *The 120 Days of Sodom* (Sade, 1987, 649). The weapon in *Catastrophe* is the projector whose glare falls on parts of the bodies or the old man's face. If the conceit of torturing a poet to make him disclose secret knowledge parodies literary criticism, staging a spectacle in which an old man looks like a living puppet parodies reality shows on television.

As a number of commentators have pointed out of the 'old grey pyjamas' that the old man is wearing despite the bitter cold (Beckett, 1986, 458), his face partly covered by a large hat and his barefoot body balancing unsteadily on top of an eighteen-inch-high block, such details cannot help but call up recent images from Abu Ghraib, the shameful reminder that the US army has used torture in the recent past to make suspected terrorists confess imputed crimes. Michael Coffey's *Samuel Beckett Is Closed* (2018) is built on such stark juxtapositions that prove Beckett's continuing relevance (see also Hickey, n.d.). One could also adduce the startling image of 'Black bag over his head' at the beginning of the short prose text 'All Strange Away' (Beckett, 1995a, 170), a text in which images of sex and torture are inextricably mixed, to argue that Beckett's imagination had a prescient quality.

In *Catastrophe*, we understand that the old man's skin has to be whitened so as to create a stronger effect from a distance; it will also erase any suggestion that this is a human face. Indeed, the director remarks disapprovingly: 'there's a trace of face' (Beckett, 1986, 459). The man must not speak either; one single projector will highlight his head when he is exhibited as a living statue or *tableau vivant* in an official meeting. The dictatorially controlled staging calls up the theatrical scenes of torture arranged every night in the Castle of Silling; the mention of 'nudity' sets a bridge between these scenes: 'Could do with more nudity' (460), the director quips. He thinks that if the old man follows his prompts, the *tableau vivant* seen by the audience will be a success. *Catastrophe*'s very title suggests more than one meaning. When the director is satisfied with the awkward pose, he says: 'There's our catastrophe. In the bag' (460). The play was first performed at the Avignon Festival in 1982 at the request of a French association defending imprisoned artists. Beckett wanted to help Václav Havel, the Czech dissident, to whom he dedicated his play. Once freed, Havel became the first democratically elected president of Czechoslovakia. At the time, charged as a subversive, he was in jail for his political work with Charter 77. Havel could only write letters once a week, and had no other paper and a pen to write; this recalls Sade's situation as we see it portrayed in *Quills*. The film begins when Sade's wife asks that ink and paper be taken away from her husband, so as to prevent him from writing obscene texts.

Beckett's Protagonist is made to strike a pose, as we often see in Sade's orgies. Becket meditates on the intersecting spaces of power and fantasy, when a perverse imagination uses people's bodies to enact an image that has to be repeated despotically. The assistant worries that the old man might want to speak, and suggests: 'What about a little ... a little ... gag?' The director explodes: 'For God's sake! This craze for explicitation! Every i dotted to death! Little gag! For God's sake!' (Beckett, 1986, 459). However, as Emilie Morin (2017) has shown, Beckett was annoyed by the too-obvious way in which Stephan Meldegg, the director of the first *Catastrophe*, presented the Protagonist all bound up in white bands (244).[26] The play's reflexive attention to dotting its i's 'to death' implies submerged puns – hence, the old man's shivers: he is frozen in order to 'freeze' in perfect petrification – and also a worry about being too explicitly political. Beckett enjoys a degree of abstraction or generalization, and wishes to leave options open. In fact, Beckett could not escape either his fame (it was useful in this case to help release Havel) or the images attached to him: in a now famous poster, he figured as a gagged 'Beckett' only two years later to denounce censorship. This play stages a structural homology between the act of staging and the act of torturing. Although we find no search for confession as in *Rough for Radio II*, *Catastrophe* insinuates that torture is limited by the director's enjoyment at producing a silly allegory, not paying heed to the fact that he forces this old man shivering in the cold to express the exact opposite of what he thinks the living statue will mean.

When the assistant is afraid that the Protagonist might lift his head, the director rejects this innovation vehemently: 'Raise his head? Where do you think we are? In Patagonia? Raise his head! For God's sake' (Beckett, 1986, 460). The geographical detail calls up the then-recent Falklands War, a conflict opposing a dictatorial Argentina sullied by a dirty war against so-called subversives and a still muscular and more powerful United Kingdom. The gesture to be avoided nevertheless happens at the end, when the Protagonist raises his head and stares at the audience. This silences applause: '*The applause falters, dies. Long pause. Fade-out of light on face*' (461).

The idea of 'catastrophe' is thus enacted at several levels. There is the exhibition of the 'catastrophe' planned by the director, the exhibition of a crippled old man on a stage as a degraded subhuman being. The Protagonist's hands twisted by disease, his bald head, and his whitened skin should make him look contemptible in a spectacle calling up the sinister Stalinian trials, with their absurd accusations and displays of broken but consenting victims. The entire system of a totalitarian regime could be called a 'catastrophe'. The spectacle it stages ends up sending back an image of its true essence; hence 'catastrophe' can be understood as the imaginary reification of a battered humanity oppressed by a perverse abuse of power.

---

[26] Morin's analysis of the play's historical context is excellent (see 2017, 239–46).

A second meaning of 'catastrophe' returns to its etymological meaning, 'reversal'. Indeed, at the very last second, the mute 'Protagonist' turns into an 'antagonist' who literally 'acts' by retrieving agency. As he lifts his head, the movement that had been forbidden, staring defiantly at the audience, this mute gesture creates the other 'catastrophe' feared by the director. As the last act in a traditional play, this single gesture has enough power to undo the rest. Here might be the root of Beckett's ethics of courage and resistance, which Badiou has often described. The etymology of 'catastrophe' is a sudden reversal, a literal 'strophe', the inner undoing of a situation perceived as theatrical. Here too, the torturer can lose his wager and be overturned by the machinery arranged for his dictatorial aims. This overturning is achieved by a minimalist gesture. The minute change at the last minute mobilizes an ethical perspective clashing with the politics of domination or oppression.

Earlier, Malone had mentioned his 'catastrophe in the ancient sense' (Beckett, 1991, 254) after he lost his stick, somewhat a 'catastrophe' for a narrator who is supposed to write the text we are reading. However, thanks to this loss, he can then speculate deeper on the meaning of the stick:

> Now that I have lost my stick I realize what it is I have lost and all it meant to me. And thence ascend, painfully, to an understanding of the Stick, shorn of all its accidents, such as I had never dreamt of. What a broadening of the mind. So that I half discern, in the veritable catastrophe that has befallen me, a blessing in disguise. How comforting that is. Catastrophe too in the ancient sense no doubt. (254)

The 'blessing in disguise' is that he will continue writing without moving from his bed, since he is stuck without a stick. 'Catastrophe' means thus any event that can be reversed as to its meaning, and the term could be seen as Beckett's variation on what Blanchot was to call 'the writing of the disaster', a term that comes close to what Beckett had in mind, even when he was turning into a political activist. This is what Blanchot writes of Sade in his book on the disaster, going back to his valuable analysis of apathy in 'Sade's Reason':

> There is nothing in Sade that can be called serious; or rather, his seriousness is the mockery of seriousness, just as *passion passes* through Sade in a moment of coolness, of secretness, of neutrality. Apathy, the infinite passivity. This is the grand irony – not Socratic, not feigned ignorance – but saturation by impropriety (when nothing whatsoever suits anymore), the grand dissimulation where all is said, all is said again and finally silenced. (Blanchot, 1986, 45)

Aristotle's *Poetics* preferred the term *peripeteia* (reversal of fortune) to 'catastrophe', but the latter would be systematized as the last act of a classical play. In *Ulysses*, Stephen Dedalus evokes the theme of banishment in Shakespeare's plays as repeating itself: 'protasis, epitasis, catastasis, catastrophe' (Joyce, 1986, 174). Beckett learned from Joyce the trick of not concluding any novel or play. The literal 'catastrophe' will be avoided by eschewing a final *dénouement*: there is no final closure or disclosure, no conclusion, no last 'turn' of the plot, because it all ends in silence, the silence that silences all the rest, and therefore keeps its ethical radicality.

Beckett's novels and plays stage bleakness, despair and post-apocalyptic situations but also suggest how to live after having confronted the catastrophe. It is a catastrophe that has already happened, to echo Donald Winnicott's posthumous paper 'Fear of Breakdown' (1974). The catastrophe is legible, as Roland Barthes contends, in any image of dead people. When looking at them, he can say: 'I shudder, like Winnicott's psychotic patient, *over a catastrophe which has already happened*' (1981, 96).

This generates another level of 'catastrophe' in which the audience is implicated. When the play was performed in Avignon and had a successful outcome by helping Havel, who was in gaol, the audience was caught up in a double bind: were they to clap at the end so as to thank Beckett and the actors, or express their solidarity with the defiant Protagonist by remaining silent? If 'catastrophe' means its very opposite and dialectically generates a 'triumph', how can one find a stable position in the face of the most significant understatement of the bold and silence stare? This quandary leads to similar questions posed by the repetitive staging of torture in *What Where*, a play exhibiting the absurdity of torture applied to obtain a confession.

If *Rough for Radio II* parodied literary criticism by showing a group of persecutors torturing a poet in a desperate effort to make him reveal an undisclosed truth, then *What Where* presents an eternal cycle of damnation in which each torturer becomes a victim in his turn. *What Where*, Beckett's last dramatic work (1983), stages a series of interrogations narrated by V or the Voice of Bam, who begins by stating: 'We are the last five' (Beckett, 1986, 470). This declaration is highly significant: in fact, we have only four characters called Bam, Bem, Bim and Bom. They occupy three positions on stage; V. remains offstage, pointing to a division of Bam into his character and his voice which calls up the structure of *Film*, in which Buster Keaton as a character is split between E (the Eye of the camera) and O (the Object of the gaze).

Bam first questions Bom about a previous interrogation conducted offstage (logically, it can only have concerned a victim named Bum). Bom tells Bam that his interrogatee divulged nothing in spite of being given the 'works'. Bam asks Bom if the victim wept, screamed and begged for mercy. Bom confirms all this, adding that the person passed out. Bam, unsatisfied with these answers, accuses Bom of lying. Bom will be given the 'works' by Bim until he confesses what was said to him. This pattern continues with Bim being interrogated by Bem, and Bem by Bam, until there is no one left to question Bam. This play features interrogations about other interrogations, creating a vertiginous spiral of questions, to be understood in the Roman or medieval sense of *quaestio*, the investigation of a witness by the means of torture. Each 'question' is loaded with unspoken echoes of its abstract semantics allied with the immediate threat of *quaestio per tormenta*. The bland use of the phrase 'give him the works' condenses in four words the thousands of pages written on the topic by Sade, who relished describing the most painful tortures. The idiom originated in the discourse of technology at the end of the nineteenth century, when it meant a complete set of parts for a machine, which sends us back to James Watt and the logics of *Watt*.

This perfect example of Beckett's minimalism is to be seen as a cog in a huge wheel that thoroughly dehumanizes subjects by a systematic use of abstraction; Bam, Bem and Bim are quasi-anonymous and undifferentiated. Nothing lets us know what the interrogation is about, except for the most basic grammatical functions: 'it', 'what' and 'where'. 'The works' has the ominous suggestion of lethal torture, since no one can be revived afterwards. V's power as Bam is absolute throughout the production (see Herren, 2002, 327). V prompts characters to appear on stage, and he halts and restarts proceedings when he is unsatisfied with how things are progressing. Bam, who remains one seat below him in the play's hierarchy of authority, serves as V's chief inquisitor, orchestrating the offstage interrogations, ordering the employment of the 'works'. V and Bam are the sole arbiters of crime, punishment, justice, freedom and the progression of events.

The action is slowed down or hurried at the discretion of V. With Bom and Bim, then Bim and Bem respectively administering the torture, it is Bam who orders it, basking in the certainty that he alone will survive. Within the tyrannical judicial system of *What Where*, torture punishes the mere suspicion of having overheard the coveted information. By torturing each interrogator for lying about the information acquired, even if there is no evidence to support the accusations, justice is reduced to a sadistic system in which all subordinates become disposable, or as Clov would say in *Endgame*, 'corpsed' (Beckett, 1986, 106) one after the other. The fact that 'Give him the works' is repeated ten times and developed into the same sequence of weeping, screaming for mercy, passing out and being unable to be revived, offers an abstract structure denouncing the perversion constituted by state torture.

Unlike the reversibility proclaimed for Pim and the narrator of *How It Is*, the dire fates of Bem, Bim and Bom follow a constant cycle, whereas immunity is granted Bam. Bam, whose name carries a faint echo of 'I am' and of the French *âme* (soul), both narrates the play and orders the torments of his subaltern accomplices, a last variation on the absolute power of the Animator and the Director. In the later works of Beckett, the tyrannical Author always retains the dubious prerogative of being the arch torturer. This arrogant and despotic solitude is also the lot of the Sadean Libertines. One of the most disquieting scenes of *Juliette* occurs at the end, when three debauched and criminal Libertines, Juliette, Clairwil and Olympia, Princess Borghese, who up to then have been accomplices in the torturing and dismembering of countless victims, decide to visit the Vesuvius volcano; no sooner have they reached the rim, than Clairwil suggests to Juliette that they should throw Olympia alive into the volcano (Sade, 1967a, 1017). The reason? They have got tired of her. They jump on her, gag her mouth, torment her for two hours, and then throw her alive into the volcano's mouth. For a while, they wait, lying tightly embraced at the rim, to see whether Olympia will be avenged by a cosmic deflagration – but nothing happens except a small eruption, which they reckon has been triggered by the fall of the body. It is then that they triumph, having 'insulted Nature' with impunity, only to realize that Nature loves being insulted because crime is her essence. However, the satanic couple of Clairwil and Juliette will not last long either. Twenty pages later, Juliette learns that Clairwil, who has been her most precious criminal mentor and devoted lesbian lover so far, has made plans to poison her that night; Juliette, tipped by the female poisoner La Durand, poisons Clairwil before she can act.

Hence the motto of *What Where*, echoed again and again by the voice of Bam, 'I am alone'. This motto applies to all Sadean heroes and heroines: their unyielding wish to consummate *jouissance* immediately, regardless of any consequence, as when Juliette sacrifices Marianne, the daughter she loves best, and helps Noirceuil throw her into a burning hearth to roast her alive, doing so apparently without any remorse (Sade, 1967a, 1187), sets them apart from all human community and even from the last shimmers of love remaining in the 'pseudo-couple' of *How It Is*. What would be Beckett's solution? By default, he appeals to the milder sadism of 'love', when each partner is ready to suffer and play the part of the victim as well as the tormentor. At least, such a martyrizing interplay offers a modicum of reversibility. In the absence of true ethical reciprocity, the possibilities offered by simple reversibility of the positions provides a weak approximation of morality, even if it is the simple nagging or mutually torturing dialogue of jealous partners that we see deployed in *Play*.[27] However, the orgasmic *jouissance* experienced time and again by Juliette will wash away and obliterate any sense of reciprocity and reversibility.

---

[27] A typical line is: 'I know what torture you must be going through, she said . . . ' (Beckett, 1986, 310).

Conclusion: Play, Pleasure and *Jouissance*

> Sade attains the end of Classical discourse and thought. . . . After him, violence, life
> and death, and sexuality will extend, below the level of representation, an immense
> expanse of shade which we are now attempting to recover, as far as we can, in our
> discourse, in our freedom, in our thought. But our thought is so brief, our freedom
> so enslaved, our discourse so repetitive, that we must face that that expanse of
> shade below is really a bottomless sea. The prosperities of *Juliette* are still more
> solitary – and endless.
>
> (Foucault, 1973, 211)

Marquis de Sade did not leave many childhood memories – he very rarely saw
his mother, which may have given him an early hatred of all mothers. However,
one vignette stands out, to be found at the beginning of *Aline and Valcour*. It
describes a game with an older child that turned sour, when little Sade was four,
the other eight; the older one was a Prince of Condé, in whose house Sade lived
with his mother, who, because she was related to the Condé family, was a lady-
in-waiting:

> one day during one of our youthful games, my vanity was ruffled because he
> disputed me the possession of one thing, to which he thought he was entitled
> from his high titles and his rank, and I avenged myself against his resistance
> with many repeated blows that I gave without any other consideration, so
> that only violent force could separate me from my adversary. (Sade, 1990,
> 403;)

This scene serves as the opening tableau of Francine Du Plessix Gray's enjoyable biography of Sade (1998, 19). Du Plessix Gray highlights the early
violence of Sade's passions, which manifested itself in his inability to let go
of an object of desire as banal as a toy. The consequences were drastic: the
young Sade was sent back to his family in the south and left to the company of
a well-read but lecherous priest.

When reading about Sade's life, Beckett may have been impressed by this
infantile inability to play, which entailed being a victim or martyr to the strength
of desire. Indeed, as psychoanalysts explain, playing entails letting go of the
object, and accepting symbolic substitutions. Later on, deprived of his sexual
objects by his repeated imprisonments, Sade was to learn the hard way how to
play – it would be by becoming a writer, but a writer who keeps enjoyment as
a goal. The horror that Sade's texts often causes is not dependent upon the
obscene or violently perverse character of the scenes described. The repetitive
style and the lack of psychological depth render the descriptions of orgies and
tortures flat and affectless; the real horror comes from the fear that these
fantasies may become reality. One's terror is that there might not be any

distinction between fantasy and real life. Thus Beckett's *Play* presents a typical lovers' triangle, a man caught up between two women who fight over him, but seen from the angle of an afterlife in Hell, a place in which these anguishing doubts and self-tortures will be eternally repeated. This corresponds to the desire expressed by Saint-Fond, one of Sade's most extreme Libertines: the wish to torture victims after their physical death. In order to achieve this, he forces his victims to sign a pact with their own blood promising to give their soul to the devil; the paper is then shoved into the anus, and the person, here called an 'object', dispatched:

> Whenever I immolate an object, whether to my ambition or to my lubricity, my desire is to make its sufferings last beyond the unending immensity of ages .... His agonies, in kind identical to those you make him endure while burying the pact, shall be everlasting; and yours will be the unspeakable delight of prolonging them beyond the limits of eternity, if eternity could have limits. (Sade, 1967a, 369–70)

Here is the site where Dante and Sade meet, if we can bring together a view of Hell as an eternity of pain, and Paradise, seen as an eternity of *jouissance*. I use the French word less because of its use by Lacan than because it is one of Sade's most recurrent terms. In French, the word combines excessive sexual enjoyment with a more legal sense of limited ownership. Sade shares this concept with one of his favourite writers, Jean-Jacques Rousseau, who had planned an essay on 'L'Art de jouir' when he was writing his *Confessions*, and whose main statement would be valid for Sade: 'When I say to myself, I have enjoyed, I still enjoy' ('En me disant, j'ai joüi, je joüis encore'; Rousseau, 1959, 1174). After I write these words on a page, *jouissance* will haunt me but also remain eternal.

There is a lesson to gain in the progression of Beckett's appreciation of Sade; first he placed Sade in Dante's company, Sade providing the key to Dante's fascination with Hell and tortures; he then began questioning the religious reading of his works, and explored the issues left by the splicing of love, justice and ethics. Finally, he saw in Sade a revolutionary writer whose irrepressible cult of energy and enjoyment would not eliminate a critical edge. In the end, for Sade, everything would be measured by a certain standard of *jouissance*, a term that does not simply indicate pleasure, but, to paraphrase *Murphy*, refers to 'such pleasure that pleasure was not the word' (Beckett, 1957, 113), a pleasure that moreover does not exclude pain.

One could argue that a concern for *jouissance* underpins *Waiting for Godot*, if we are ready to accept that 'waiting for Godot' does not mean 'waiting for God', a religious interpretation rejected by Beckett – in spite of the constant references to Jesus and the Bible in the play – but signifies 'waiting for *jouissance*'. Should one remain sceptical about this interpretation, one could adduce textual proof from Dante. Dante's sublime vision condensed in the last Canto of *Paradiso* offers a version of what the name 'Godot' or even Mr Knott's name might suggest. At that point, Dante the poet perceives the unity of the universe as it is contained in a knot (*nodo*). This contemplation triggers an unspeakable joy, a joy so strong that joy would not be quite the word. What's more, this *jouissance* keeps on growing each time the poet mentions it. And we can add that it grows every time we repeat it with him:

> La forma universal di questo nodo
> credo ch'i' vidi, perché più di largo,
> dicendo questo, mi sento ch'i' godo.
> (*Paradiso*, Canto XXXIII: 91–3; Dante Alighieri, 1967, 807)

Burton Raffel translates:

> I think I must have seen the universal
> Form of this great knot, for my joy increases
> Simply because I hear myself saying this.
> (Dante Alighieri, 2010, 512)

A more literal rendering might be:

> The universal form of that knot
> methinks I saw, because increasingly,
> As I say this, I sense that I am full of joy.

Can we follow Beckett's darkest texts to the end, at least until they yield an intimation of ineffable joy? A first step on the way would entail deleting the final 't' in Godot . . . '*Waiting for Godo*' would pun on the tool so often used by Sade's Libertines, the huge dildo called in French *godemichet*, or in slang, *gode*. We will remember that in Paris, in Beckett's time, rue Godot de Mauroy was well known for its sex shops and brothels.[28] Unlike Mick Jagger, who gave an anthem to his generation with his famous 'I can't get no satisfaction', Beckett's debunks the modern *taedium vitae* by forcing us to absorb a strong Sadean remedy, even if the brew tastes foul at times, when he tells us: 'Frenchmen and women, Irishmen, Irish women, and all of you, another effort if you want to enjoy!'

---

[28] This gives more salt to the anecdote narrated by A. J. Leventhal, Beckett's old friend from Dublin, to Deirdre Bair about a prostitute who had asked Beckett, who, when solicited, passed by, whether he was 'waiting for Godot' (Bair, 1978, 382). Here, I am also alluding to the famous title of Sade's main pamphlet, 'Yet Another Effort, Frenchmen, If You Want to Become Republican' (Sade, 1965, 296–339).

Works Cited

Albright, Daniel (2003). *Beckett and Aesthetics*. Cambridge, UK: Cambridge University Press.

Allen, William S. (2018). *Without End: Sade's Critique of Reason*. New York: Bloomsbury.

Apollinaire, Guillaume (1909, republished 2014). *L'Œuvre du Marquis de Sade*. Paris: Jude Kahn.

Artaud, Antonin (2004). 'Le Théâtre de la Cruauté: Premier Manifeste', in *Oeuvres*, ed. Evelyne Grossman. Paris: Gallimard (Quarto).

Badiou, Alain (2003). *On Beckett*, eds. and trans. Nina Power and Alberto Toscano, Manchester: Clinamen Press.

Bair, Deirdre (1978). *Samuel Beckett: A Biography*. New York: Simon and Schuster.

Barthes, Roland (1976). *Sade, Fourier, Loyola*, trans. Richard Miller. New York: Farrar, Straus and Giroux.

(1981). *Camera Lucida*, trans. Richard Howard. New York: Noonday Press.

Bataille, Georges (1985) [1930]. 'The Use Value of D. A. F. de Sade (An Open Letter to My Comrades)', in *Visions of Excess: Selected Writings 1927–1939*, ed. and trans. Allan Stoekl. Minneapolis, MN: University of Minnesota Press.

Beckett, Samuel (1953). *Watt*. New York: Grove Press.

(1957). *Murphy*. New York: Grove Press.

(1961). *Comment c'est*. Paris: Editions de Minuit.

(1964). *How It Is*. New York: Grove Press.

(1970). *Proust*, and *Three Dialogues*. London: Calder.

(1974). *Mercier and Camier*. New York: Grove Press.

(1983). *Disjecta*, ed. Ruby Cohn. New York: Grove Press.

(1986). *The Complete Dramatic Works*. London: Faber and Faber.

(1991). *Three Novels*. New York: Grove Press.

(1992). *Dream of Fair to Middling Women*. Dublin: The Black Cat Press.

(1995a). *The Complete Short Prose 1929–1989*, ed. S. E. Gontarski. New York: Grove Press.

(1995b). *Eleutheria*. Paris: Editions de Minuit.

(1996). *Eleutheria*, trans. Barbara Wright. London: Faber and Faber.

(1999). *Beckett's Dream Notebook*, ed. John Pilling. Reading, UK: Beckett International Foundation.

(2009). *The Letters of Samuel Beckett, Vol. I: 1929–1940*, eds. Martha Fehsenfeld and Lois More Overbeck. Cambridge: Cambridge University Press.

(2011). *The Letters of Samuel Beckett, Vol. II: 1941–1956*, eds. George Craig, Martha Fehsenfeld, Dan Gunn and Lois More Overbeck. Cambridge: Cambridge University Press.

(2012). 'Text 3', in *The Collected Poems*, eds. Seán Lawlor and John Pilling. London: Faber and Faber.

(2014). *The Letters of Samuel Beckett, Vol. III: 1957–1965*, eds. George Craig, Martha Fehsenfeld, Dan Gunn and Lois More Overbeck. Cambridge: Cambridge University Press.

(2016). *The Letters of Samuel Beckett, Vol. IV: 1966–1989*, eds. George Craig, Martha Fehsenfeld, Dan Gunn and Lois More Overbeck. Cambridge: Cambridge University Press.

Bersani, Leo and Ulysse Dutoit (1993). *Arts of Impoverishment: Beckett, Rothko, Resnais*. Cambridge, MA: Harvard University Press.

Blanchot, Maurice (1986). *The Writing of the Disaster*, trans. Ann Smock. Lincoln, NE: University of Nebraska Press.

(1995). 'Sade's Reason', in *The Maurice Blanchot Reader*, ed. Michael Holland. Oxford: Blackwell, pp. 74–100.

Borges, Jorge Luis (1998). 'Tlön, Uqbar, Orbis Tertius', in *Collected Fictions*, trans. Andrew Hurley. New York: Penguin.

Boulter, Jonathan (2012). '"We Have Our Being in Justice": Samuel Beckett's *How It Is*', in *Samuel Beckett and Pain*, eds. Mariko Hori Tanaka, Yoshiki Tajiri and Michiko Tsushima. Amsterdam: Rodopi, pp. 173–200.

Breton, André (1969). *Manifestoes of Surrealism*, trans. Richard Seaver and Helen R. Lane. Ann Arbor, MI: The University of Michigan Press.

Carter, Angela (1978). *The Sadeian Woman*. London: Virago.

Caselli, Daniela (2005). *Beckett's Dantes: Intertextuality in the Fiction and Criticism*. Manchester: Manchester University Press.

Coffey, Michael (2018). *Samuel Beckett Is Closed*. New York: Foxrock Books.

Cunningham, David (2008). '"We Have Our Being in Justice": Formalism, Abstraction and Beckett's "Ethics"', in *Beckett and Ethics*, ed. Russell Smith. London: Continuum, pp. 21–37.

Dante Alighieri (1967). *Opere*, ed. Fredi Chiapelli. Milan: Murcia.

(1981). *The Divine Comedy of Dante Alighieri*, trans. Allen Mandelbaum. New York: Bantam.

(2010). *The Divine Comedy*, trans. Burton Raffel. Evanston, IL: Northwestern University Press.

Delon, Michel (1990). 'Introduction', in Marquis de Sade, *Oeuvres*, Volume I. Paris: Gallimard (Pléiade), pp. ix–lviii.

Du Plessix Gray, Francine (1998). *At Home with the Marquis de Sade: A Life*. New York: Simon and Schuster.

Foucault, Michel (1973). *The Order of Things: An Archeology of the Human Sciences*. New York: Vintage.

Friedman, Alan Warren (2018). *Surreal Beckett: Samuel Beckett, James Joyce and Surrealism*. New York: Routledge.

Gontarski, S. E. (2018). *Revisioning Beckett: Samuel Beckett's Decadent Turn*. New York: Bloomsbury.

Gorer, Geoffrey (1934). *The Revolutionary Ideas of the Marquis de Sade*. London: Wishart & Co.

(1955). 'The Pornography of Death', *Encounter*, 5 (October), 49–52.

Heine, Maurice (1950). *Le Marquis de Sade*. Paris: Gallimard.

Herren, Graley (2002). 'Facing the Darkness: Interrogations Across Genre in Samuel Beckett's "What Where."' *Midwest Quarterly*, 43(3), 322–36.

Hickey, Kenneth (n. d.). 'Give Him the Works: Torture in Beckett's Late Plays', *An Academic Life*. https://kennethjhickey.wordpress.com/theatre-film /give-him-the-works-torture-in-becketts-late-plays/

Horkheimer, Max, and Theodor W. Adorno (2002). *Dialectic of the Enlightenment*, trans. Edmund Jephcott. Stanford, CA: Stanford University Press.

Joyce, James (1986). *Ulysses*, ed. Hans Walter Gabler. New York: Random House.

Kant, Immanuel (1996). *Practical Philosophy*, trans. Mary J. Gregor. Cambridge, UK: Cambridge University Press.

Klossowski, Pierre (1991). *Sade My Neighbor*, trans. Alphonso Lingis. Evanston, IL: Northwestern University Press.

(2001) [1933]. 'Éléments d'une étude psychanalytique sur le marquis de Sade', in *Écrits d'un monomane: Essais 1933–1939*, ed. Pierre Klossowski. Paris: Le Promeneur.

Knowlson, James (1996). *Damned to Fame: The Life of Samuel Beckett*. New York: Simon and Schuster.

Lacan, Jacques (2006). *Ecrits*, trans. Bruce Fink. New York: Norton.

Lafourcade, Georges (1928). *La Jeunesse de Swinburne (1837–1867)*. Paris: Les Belles Lettres.

Le Brun, Annie (2014). *Attaquer le soleil*. Paris: Musée d'Orsay and Gallimard.

Leopardi, Giacomo (2011). *Canti*, trans. Jonathan Galassi. New York: Farrar, Straus and Giroux.

Marty, Eric (2011). *Pourquoi le XXe siècle a-t-il pris Sade au sérieux?* Paris: Seuil.

McMillan, Douglas, and Martha Fehsenfeld (1988). *Beckett in the Theatre*. New York: Riverrun Press.

Morin, Emilie (2017). *Beckett's Political Imagination*. Cambridge, UK: Cambridge University Press.

Murat, Laure (2014). *The Man Who Thought He Was Napoleon: Toward a Political History of Madness*, trans. Deke Dusinberre. Chicago: Chicago University Press.

Murphy, P. J. (1994). 'Beckett and the Philosophers', in *The Cambridge Companion to Beckett*, ed. John Pilling. Cambridge: Cambridge University Press, pp. 222–40.

Pilling, John (2014). 'BECKETT/SADE: Texts for Nothing', in *The Edinburgh Companion to Samuel Beckett and the Arts*, ed. S. E. Gontarski. Edinburgh: Edinburgh University Press, pp. 117–30.

Praz, Mario (1948) [1930]. *La carne, la morte e il diavolo; nella letteratura romantica*. Florence: Sansoni Editore.

Proust, Marcel (1987). *A la recherche du temps perdu*, ed. Jean-Yves Tadié, Vol. I. Paris: Gallimard (Pléiade).

(2002). *Swann's Way*, trans. Lydia Davis. New York: Viking.

Rabaté, Jean-Michel (2016). *Think, Pig!* New York: Fordham University Press.

Rousseau, Jean-Jacques (1959). 'Art de jouir et autres fragments', in *Oeuvres complètes I* (*Les Confessions et autres textes autobiographiques*), ed. B. Gagnebin. Paris: Gallimard (Pléiade).

Sade, Marquis de (1965). *Justine, Philosophy in the Bedroom, and Other Writings*, trans. Richard Seaver and Austryn Wainhouse. New York: Grove Weidenfeld.

(1967a). *Histoire de Juliette ou Les Prospérités du vice*, in *Oeuvres complètes*, vol. XXIV. Paris: Jean-Jacques Pauvert.

(1967b). *La Nouvelle Justine, ou les Malheurs de la vertu*, in *Oeuvres complètes*, vol. VI. Paris: Jean-Jacques Pauvert.

(1987). *The 120 Days of Sodom*, trans. Austryn Wainhouse and Richard Seaver. New York: Grove Press.

(1990). *Aline et Valcour*, in *Oeuvres I*, ed. Michel Delon. Paris: Gallimard (Pléiade).

St. Jorre, John de (1994). *Venus Bound: The Erotic Voyage of the Olympia Press and Its Writers*. New York: Random House.

Schopenhauer, Arthur (1969). *The World as Will and Representation*, trans. E. F. J. Payne. New York: Dover.

Trahan, Michaël (2017). *La Postérité du scandale. Petite histoire de la réception de Sade (1909–1939)*. Montreal: Nota Bene.

Van Hulle, Dirk, and Mark Nixon (2013). *Samuel Beckett's Library*. Cambridge, UK: Cambridge University Press.

Weiss, Peter (1981). *The Persecution and Assassination of Jean-Paul Marat, As Performed by the Inmates of the Asylum of Charenton under the Direction of the Marquis de Sade*, trans. Geoffrey Skelton and Adrian Mitchell. Long Grove, IL: Waveland Press.

Winnicott, Donald W. (1974). 'Fear of Breakdown', ed. Clare Winnicott, *International Review of Psychoanalysis*, 1, 103–7.

Cambridge Elements ≡

Beckett Studies

Dirk Van Hulle
University of Oxford
Dirk Van Hulle is Professor of Bibliography and Modern Book History
at the University of Oxford and director of the Centre for Manuscript
Genetics at the University of Antwerp.

Mark Nixon
University of Reading
Mark Nixon is Associate Professor in Modern Literature at the University
of Reading and the Co-Director of the Beckett International Foundation.

About the Series
This series presents cutting-edge research by distinguished and emerging scholars, providing space for the most relevant debates informing Beckett studies as well as neglected aspects of his work. In times of technological development, religious radicalism,
unprecedented migration, gender fluidity, environmental and social crisis, Beckett's
works find increased resonance. Elements in Beckett Studies is a key resource for readers
interested in the current state of the field.

Cambridge Elements ≡

Beckett Studies

Printed in the United States
By Bookmasters